# SHE NEVER FAILED ME
## *Lucinda Burbank Morton*

## INDIANA'S FIRST LADY *of the* CIVIL WAR

CAROLYN LAFEVER

winterspublishing.com

*She Never Failed Me: Lucinda Burbank Morton*
*Indiana's First Lady of the Civil War*





Published by:
Winters Publishing
P.O. Box 501
Greensburg, IN 47240
812-663-4948
www.winterspublishing.com



Printed in the United States of America.

ISBN: 978-1-954116-27-6
Library of Congress Control Number: 2024937422

# DEDICATION

To My Helpers and Encouragers

Karen Lawson, Bonny Kerkhof,

and

Dr. A. James Fuller

Thank you for the many hours you spent reading about Lucinda and helping me tell her story.

# TABLE OF CONTENTS

# TABLE OF CONTENTS

## PART 3: Mrs. Senator Morton



## PART 4: Widow Morton

# INTRODUCTION

I was working on an exhibit for the Mansion House Museum, 214 E. Main Street, in Centerville, Indiana. The shelves and drawers needed dusting and some new things added for the exhibit. The large lower drawers of the built-in cabinet had not been fully cleaned out and I decided to dig a little deeper. There might be something I could use.

I thought we had looked in every nook and cranny of the old historic house museum, but to my surprise, I found a large, old framed photograph of a woman in the lowest drawer. The gold frame was beautiful but it was broken at the corner. I had no idea who the woman was until I looked on the back. The writing said Lucinda Morton, 80 years old. This was the wife of Oliver P. Morton, the Civil War Governor of Indiana.

The story of Oliver P. Morton, Indiana Governor and U.S. Senator, has been told many times in newspapers, books, and essays. There have been many statues of him placed in his home state and other places, including the Wayne County Courthouse, Richmond, Indiana. A statue of Morton stands in Statuary Hall in Washington, along with another Indiana great, Lew Wallace. There was much to say about Morton as his speeches and activities were in the newspapers from the earliest days of his career. Loved by many and hated by his opponents, Oliver Morton charged ahead, never minding if his opinions caused controversy. All through his years of public service, his companion for forty-three years was his wife, Lucinda Burbank Morton. With all the large amount of written material generated by his career, she was rarely mentioned in the accounts of Morton's life.

Lucinda Burbank married Oliver P. Morton in 1843. Lucinda had known Oliver since their school days. Her father owned a thriving business and the family were prominent members of the Centerville community. They were well acquainted and she knew him as a strong, intelligent, vibrant man that would challenge her to keep up with him.

Lucinda was a woman of her time in making her home her main concern, but better educated than most women in the 1830s–1840s. She was interested in all the things that interested Oliver. She made their home a refuge from his ambitious and restless lifestyle. She was calm, patient, and tactful, whereas Oliver loved to debate and was not unwilling to irritate those who opposed him.

I wanted to learn more about Lucinda when I found the large photograph of her. It had originally been given to the old Centerville Library. The library was moved into the newly remodeled building in 1999. The remodeled building was originally built in 1867 as the Wayne County Sheriff's residence and Jail. Centerville was the Wayne County Seat of Justice from 1816–1873. The new library gave the photograph with the broken frame to the Mansion House. And since the ornate gold frame of Lucinda's picture was damaged, it had been put away in a large drawer. Pictures of Lucinda are rare and this was a treasure. The Mansion House had the frame restored and the faded, gray matting replaced to brighten the picture. It now hangs on the wall by the side of a painting of Oliver Morton in the Mansion House front parlor.

There are no books, but there are many newspaper articles about Lucinda. There are two outstanding biographies of Oliver P. Morton that are excellent and detailed. The first is by William Dudley Foulke, a two-volume work titled *Life of Oliver P. Morton, Including His Important Speeches,* published in 1898. The second is by A. James Fuller, author of *Oliver P. Morton and the Politics of the Civil War and Reconstruction,* published in 2017. Dr. Fuller included more about Lucinda than any other Morton biographers. His extensive footnotes have been a helpful resource about her while Oliver was in the U.S. Senate.

It turned out that Lucinda played a larger part in Oliver's success as Governor and Senator than she was given credit. She kept their home in Indianapolis, yet traveled to Washington with Oliver as often as she could. He regularly wrote to her about his political life and she wrote almost every day when they were apart. Their children were not neglected as they spent time with relatives when their parents had to be away and they often visited in Washington. When Oliver's stroke in 1865 caused disability and paralysis, a larger burden was placed on Lucinda for the rest of their married life, but apparently she handled it with strength and grace.

Lucinda had her own times of illness and disability. Victorian medicine was limited in being able to help. Oliver would not give up his political life in spite of much pain and suffering. Both Oliver and Lucinda looked past their restrictions and continued to travel, to maintain residences in Washington and Indianapolis, and to nurture their sons. Their many friends and close family members aided them with love and support through good times and bad.

Lucinda was a woman of Christian faith. She attended worship services as often as she could. When a youngster, Oliver had been forced to sit long, dull hours in church with his aunts and grandparents. His past experience seemed to cause him to be less patient about attending church services. But Oliver knew his Bible and often used illustrations in his speeches. He supported his wife and others in their faith.

Lucinda and Oliver Morton had a marriage of compatibility and love. Their three sons felt their love as it was lavishly given to them. Throughout all the times of illness, difficulty, and dramatic events, Lucinda and Oliver came through them together, only to become stronger. When Oliver was on his deathbed with Lucinda so faithfully attending him, he said, "In all these years of sickness, she has never failed me."

*A wife of noble character who can find?*
*She is worth far more than rubies.*
*Her husband has full confidence in her*
*And lacks nothing of value.*
*She brings him good, not harm,*
*All the days of her life.*

Proverbs 31:10–12 (NIV)

# Part 1

# THE CENTERVILLE YEARS

# Chapter 1

# LUCINDA MARIA BURBANK

"The excitement following the firing on Fort Sumter in April 1861 was doubtless the most intense that Indianapolis ever knew," recalled Lucinda Morton, the wife of Indiana's Civil War Governor, Oliver P. Morton. "There were many other times of excitement in the days of 1861 to 1865, but nothing to equal that occasioned by the firing on Fort Sumter." Mrs. Morton recounted her memories as Indiana's Civil War First Lady at a meeting of the Daughters of the American Revolution in 1905.

Lucinda Morton became the First Lady of Indiana in January 1861 upon the inauguration of her husband, Governor Oliver P. Morton. No one could have predicted the difficulties that she would face while her husband was Governor of Indiana. Lucinda had already become used to Oliver's turbulent political career. She had spent over fifteen years with him in Centerville. As Oliver's law career grew and prospered, his involvement in politics drew him more and more into public recognition. Lucinda was a steadfast and supportive influence. She was his efficient, faithful, and loving companion. When Morton became Governor, the couple began a life of unimaginable challenges brought to Indiana by the American Civil War.

Lucinda Burbank was born on May 16, 1825, in York Township, Adams County, Pennsylvania, to Isaac Burbank and Mary Elizabeth

Burbank. Isaac Burbank (1788–1876), Lucinda's father, was born in Bethel, Windsor County, Vermont. Isaac had received a good education and at age eighteen, he began teaching school in Hanover, Pennsylvania. He did so well that he was put in charge of the schools at Emmetsburg, Maryland, for which he received what was considered a lucrative salary. It was while teaching in Emmetsburg that he met and married one of his students, Mary Elizabeth Troxell (1799–1883), in 1819. Although Isaac was earning a good living in Pennsylvania as a teacher, he decided to change his profession and look for new opportunities in the west. Shortly after Lucinda's birth in 1825, the Burbank family, with two young children and the baby, made their way west to Indiana, the land of new opportunities on the western frontier.

The road to the Indiana Territory through Ohio was not much more than a wide trail. It was muddy when rainy, dusty when dry, and always rough and difficult. Settlers had come into the present day Wayne County from the eastern and southern states as early as 1805–1807. The first area that had been opened by the Government on the western frontier was in a section of the Indiana Territory called The Gore, a small, elongated, triangular-shaped area in east central Indiana, just west of the Ohio border. The Gore was formed in 1795 as part of the Treaty of Greenville settlement made between the United States and the Indian Confederation. The last to sign the treaty was Little Turtle, Chief of the Miami people.

In 1809, the Twelve-Mile Purchase in Indiana was obtained as a settlement made by the Fort Wayne Treaty between the Government and the Native Americans. This land was west of, and parallel to, the Greenville Treaty Line, making more land available for purchase in the new Indiana Territory. This encouraged more people to move into the area. The western border of the Treaty Line was located about the center of the present Cambridge City. This extended area in Indiana was given the name of Wayne County in 1810, by the Indiana Territorial Legislature.

*(Above) An Indiana map and (right) a Wayne County map.*

With the population growing, it was time to form a governing body for the county. Wayne County commissioners and other officials were appointed and the site of the first village of Salisbury was selected. The town was just south of the crossroads of Salisbury Road and the National Road (U.S. 40), west of Richmond. Wayne County was part of the Indiana Territory until 1816 when Indiana became a state.

The Isaac Burbank family arrived in Indiana in early 1826,

traveling west on the Cumberland Road, later known as the National Road. The road had not been finished much farther west than Wheeling, West Virginia. The National Road was planned to eventually go from Cumberland, Maryland to Springfield, Illinois. It was not until 1827 that the road was completely surveyed and construction began in Indiana. The road into Indiana passed through heavy wooded areas and waterways. Travel was by walking, on horseback, or in strong wagons. The weary Burbank family bypassed Richmond and decided to settle in Centerville (Centreville—old spelling), the county seat of Indiana's Wayne County since 1816. At that time, the town's population was about 400.

Wayne County's first village and the Wayne County Seat of Justice of Salisbury was platted in 1812. Centerville, platted in 1814, was the second village. Centerville became the second Wayne County Seat of Justice in 1816, approved by the first Indiana State Legislature. The site for Salisbury was about six miles west of the Ohio border. It

*This monument erected by the Daughters of the American Revolution in 1924 marks the site of Salisbury, the first county seat of Wayne County. The town no longer exists. It also marks the boundary line between Government lands and Indian lands and the birthplace of Oliver P. Morton, Governor of Indiana during the Civil War.*

was selected to be the first county seat over the objection of settlers who lived farther west, and who believed the county seat should be nearer the center of the expanding county. By 1816, residents of Centerville were able to exert enough political pressure at the new State Legislature to have the county seat removed from Salisbury to Centerville. It took a few years of negotiations, lawsuits, and various stalling tactics before the county business was completely moved to Centerville. Some of the elected officials who had served at Salisbury refused to move and resigned. However, Centerville prospered, as new business was established and professional offices moved to the new county seat.

Isaac Burbank's first business in Centerville was with Samuel Booker. Booker was one of the first to establish a general mercantile store in Centerville. Their business was in a log house built on the site of the American House, located on the southwest corner of Main Street and Cross Street (Morton Avenue). In 1838, Burbank moved to Cambridge City and was in business there for eighteen months. He moved back to Centerville where he set up a thriving general

*Location of Isaac Burbank's store on Main Street in Centerville, Indiana, circa 1902. Courtesy of Historic Centerville.*

mercantile on East Main Street. The store was in a choice spot across the street from the Courthouse and on the heavily traveled National Road. An 1840 list of Centerville businesses shows Isaac's business as "dry goods, groceries, carriages, and buggies." The store building is still standing at 113 East Main Street.

Isaac Burbank was a well-respected businessman. His mercantile flourished and he became wealthy. Centerville was a busy town with people coming to do business at the Courthouse, do their shopping and trading, and to meet the stagecoach. The stagecoach brought mail, passengers, and the latest news from the east.

The 1840s–1850s were busy years of emigration to the expanding western frontier. Hundreds of travelers came through on Centerville's Main Street (the National Road) during the warm weather months. When cold weather came, the traffic slowed down. This was the main road from east to west and the first Federal Government-sponsored road. It had officially opened through Indiana in 1834, when the double covered bridge over the Whitewater River was completed at Richmond. Every type of traffic moved over this early road, including horse or oxen-drawn vehicles of all kinds. Covered wagons, sometimes with droves of livestock, were a daily sight going through town. It was the main road from the Ohio border west through Indiana until the 1960s and the building of I-70, an interstate highway a few miles north. Since the National Road was the best road east and west through central Indiana, heavy traffic continued to move over it for decades.

The Burbank store was kept well stocked for local trade and travelers. The store carried everything from food, hardware for travelers and farmers, materials for clothing, and about anything a customer might need. For a time, Isaac kept a livery stable with supplies for stabling horses. A purchase invoice dated October 10, 1832 lists among Isaac's purchases, tea and one bag of coffee (beans), both expensive products. Other purchases were bolts of dark print fabrics, various blue prints, and sewing supplies. The school term was in session, so he ordered one-half dozen pasteboards (slates) and one dozen spellers. The total cost on the invoice was $99.59. In order to help pay for the supplies, he traded 35 pounds of feathers, 5 barrels of flour, 44 dozen eggs, 20 yards of linsey (linen cloth woven from flax), and a few other items. The difference Isaac had to pay was $43.98. He added a few more items he had forgotten to order that added up to his final cost of $59.35.

There was very little cash money available, so much of the trading by merchants and their customers was by barter. The ladies would make thread or yarn with their spinning wheels and cloth of wool or linen on their looms. They brought in extra eggs, milk products, and baked goods that were used for trade or for credit for the next purchases. Merchants would trade for rags, feathers, ginseng and herbs from the woods, and flour or corn meal from the farmers. It was only when products were shipped to Cincinnati by freight wagon, a trip made with a drove of livestock, or goods sent by boat on the new Whitewater Canal, that there might be payment in cash money.

Isaac Burbank and William Widup, a maker of hats, were among the leading merchants in town. In 1837, when the contract fell through for grading and paving four blocks of Centerville's Main Street, Burbank and Widup took over the paving contract. The costs for paving were shared by the Federal Government and the town. The contract was for $7,500.

The stone paving blocks were from one to two feet long, six inches thick, and a foot wide. The stone was local, quarried out of Lick Creek, southeast of Centerville. The stonecutters finished the blocks "as smooth as building stone," according to local newspapers. The stones were laid with careful precision, chinked, planed off, and finished to a level that was consistent with the road entering the town.

The job of laying paving stones was so well done that for over three-quarters of a century, all types of horse-drawn vehicles, hundreds of covered wagons, stagecoaches, freight wagons, horses, and other livestock traveled over it. Although it lasted many years, the pavement became rough and the stones loose and worn down, until it became one of the roughest stretches of the National Road in eastern Indiana. With the coming of automobiles, road improvements were necessary, and the old road was replaced. This early work was the first "paved" section of the National Road in Indiana.

*National Road mile marker, located along National Road, 3 miles west of Centerville. Markers like this were placed one mile apart to aid travelers. This marker was put in place after 1836, when Cambridge City was founded. The marker shows the distance to the next town(s) and the state line. This marker indicates it is 13 miles to the Indiana/Ohio state line, 6 miles to Cambridge City, and 3 miles to Centerville.*

The Burbank family grew to include seven children, three sons and four daughters. Isaac's obituary speaks of two other children who died in infancy. The family of children included Rachael Elmira, born 1819; Jacob Edward, born 1822; Lucinda Maria, born 1825; John Albyne, born 1827; Joseph Henry, born 1833; Eliza, born 1834; and Sarah, born 1840. The family first lived in rental houses, but as business flourished, Isaac purchased his own home. When Lucinda was married in 1845, the Burbank family lived in the apartment above the Main Street store. Additions had been built at the back of the building for the family and for business storage.

# Chapter 2

# CENTERVILLE IN 1840

The Centerville where Lucinda Burbank and Oliver Morton grew up is best described by the visit of twenty-three-year-old John Parsons of Petersburg, Virginia in 1840. Parsons came for an extended visit to Indiana after having completed his education in 1839, graduating from the University of Virginia. Parsons planned to tour the western states and to visit a cousin who had settled in Wabash County, Indiana.

*John Parsons.*

Parsons' detailed diary, *A Tour Through Indiana in 1840*, published in book form in 1920, describes his trip. His first stop was at Wheeling, West Virginia. There he took a steamboat to Cincinnati. He continued on the Ohio River to Madison, Indiana, spending some time there. He boarded a train north to Vernon—the county seat of Jennings County—where he spent several days.

From Vernon, Parsons traveled north by stagecoach to Brookville. The road the stage traveled was rough and often was "corduroyed." Parsons described the corduroy road as "Ten-foot rails are made of good timber, oak or ash, split wide and laid close together across the grade with a little soil thrown on the rails to level up and hold them in place." He continued, "I was soon to learn the sensation, first of rapid travel along a comparatively smooth stretch of level upland, a swift descent of a steep hillside, then the indescribable bump, bump, bump of the vehicle as the wheels leap jarringly from one log to the next." Parsons wondered if the trip would have been smoother if he had ridden horseback instead of taking the stagecoach.

At one stagecoach stop at an inn, a large "army" of porkers or hogs passed along the stagecoach road. The drove of hogs was estimated to number from two to three thousand. It would take from ten days to three weeks, according to the condition of the road, to drive the animals from Wayne County farms to the Cincinnati market where they were sold.

Parsons spent a few days at Brookville before he again boarded the stage, riding north over similar rough roads to Centerville. His traveling companion on this trip was Robert Dale Owen, one of the founders of New Harmony, Indiana. Owens managed the day-to-day operation of the socialistic, utopian community in southern Indiana. He was a politician and prolific writer. Parsons did not expect to find so much education or refinement in Indiana. The state was portrayed in eastern newspapers as uneducated, backward, and uncouth. But he was pleasantly surprised at what he found in Madison and other towns on the way north.

The description of the roads, the droves of animals on the road, the hospitality and friends Parsons found along the way, are a picture of travel in the state as well as an important description of Centerville in 1840.

John Parsons arrived safely in Centerville on the stagecoach. His impression of the town was one of admiration. "I confess I was much impressed with this place when I first beheld it from the stage, and later when walking about its streets. The town is level, said to be healthy, and surrounded by fine farming land. It contains mills and machinery of various descriptions, several mercantile stores, three taverns, several physicians and lawyers, a printing office, a seminary, and as I was told, a large number of mechanics of almost all descriptions."

Parsons met several men while lodging at the Lashley Tavern, a favorite meeting place for travelers and men of the town. He became acquainted with lawyers James Rariden, Judge Charles H. Test, John D. Newman, Jacob Julian, and his younger brother, George W. Julian, who became Parsons' favorite companion. Those mentioned and others he met were to become important men in Wayne County and Indiana history.

The second morning of his stay, Parsons observed a joint celebration of the scholars of Miss Sarah Dickinson and Mr. and Mrs. George Rea. They were students, both boys and girls, of the Wayne County Seminary, who formed a procession and marched to the Methodist Church. They were attending an address made by John R. Stitt. Lucinda would have probably been a part of the school group.

Parsons wrote in his diary, "… I perceived that the atmosphere of Centerville savored not at all of the backwoods, and that both literature and the arts flourished most amazingly."

In the evening, Parsons attended the Dark Lyceum that was held in the Courthouse. It was a program of debate between young lawyers who were practicing their speaking and debating skills. He stated that he found this entertainment of greater interest than any he had encountered in the western country. "Wilderness I shall of a certainly not call it, for that would be a misnomer. Seat of culture would be a better name for this town, with its academics and school, and its men and women of culture and refinement."

The whole town seemed to be in attendance at the Courthouse debate, including pretty young ladies. The debating society usually met on the second floor of the Seminary building, but because of the

*(Above) The old Centerville Courthouse on Main Street, built in 1832. Pen and ink drawing by Jack Phelps.*

*(Above) The old Courthouse with the bell tower removed. Looking east on Main Street, at the corner of Main Street and Cross (Morton) Street, in Centerville, Indiana, circa 1910. Courtesy of Historic Centerville.*

crowd size, it met in the brick Courthouse on the northeast corner of Main and Main Cross Streets (Morton Avenue). Parsons met several other prominent people there, including Mr. Isaac Burbank, Lucinda's father.

Mr. Parsons' description of Centerville and Richmond sheds great light on the atmosphere and life in Wayne County of the 1840s, when both Lucinda Burbank and Oliver Morton were growing up there. Unfortunately, young Parsons became ill and died on his way home, but his diary was preserved and published many years after his death.

It is important to note that Wayne County was the wealthiest and the largest by population in Indiana in 1840. The census of 1830 shows Wayne County with a population of 18,589. In this census, while Indiana still had many illiterate citizens, Wayne County had only 42 people over 20 years old who were not able to read and write.

# Chapter 3

# WAYNE COUNTY SEMINARY

Lucinda Burbank and Oliver Morton both attended the Wayne County Seminary in Centerville, a few blocks south of Main Street on School Street. It was established in 1827, and opened its doors in October 1829. All of the Burbank children were able to attend and complete

*Wayne County Seminary. The building was sold and renamed twice before becoming the Centerville Public School, circa 1870. Courtesy of Historic Centerville.*

their education there. While many higher education (Seminaries) schools were only for boys, in an announcement in the *Richmond Palladium,* December 26, 1835, the Trustees of the Wayne County Seminary encouraged those citizens "who know and appreciate the worth of a good education … to place their sons, daughters, and wards within the institution." Also listed were the teachers, tuition costs, and classes that included spelling, reading, penmanship, arithmetic, grammar, history, bookkeeping, geography, algebra, geometry, surveying, natural and moral philosophy, astronomy, and Latin and Greek languages. The school offered elementary to collegiate level classes for male and female students. Both of Lucinda's parents were well educated and they made sure their children took advantage of the education available in Centerville.

Many early settlers in Wayne County were of the Friends faith, also known as Quakers. The seating for men and women was separated in their worship service, but everyone was encouraged to speak (as the Spirit led them) in the service. Women were considered to be equal with men. The Friends or Quakers soon established their own schools. Girls received the same basic education as boys. Friends' schools ended at the eighth grade. The Wayne County Seminary provided higher education opportunities for boys and girls, including Quaker children, if they chose and could afford it. However, the Quakers wanted a place to educate their children that was focused more on religious education than the Seminary offered. Earlham School in Richmond was founded in 1847, as a boarding school for the religious education of Quaker adolescents. In 1849, it became Earlham College when collegiate studies were added.

The October 25, 1843 *Wayne County Record* reported on the progress of a new addition to the building and about the organization of the Wayne County Seminary. By this time, Lucinda may have finished her education.

The Wayne County Seminary charged tuition and students who did not live nearby could board with local families. Only parents who could handle the tuition enrolled their children. The seminary averaged about 60 students per session with two sessions a year. There were seminaries in other counties, but the girls and boys who attended the Wayne County Seminary were considered especially well educated.

In 1836, Samuel Hoshour began teaching at the Seminary. His outstanding qualities as an educator attracted attention across the state. Parents took note and sent their children to study under him. He left the school after four years and moved to nearby Cambridge City where he headed its new Seminary. Hoshour later was appointed a

*Samuel Hoshour, educator, pastor, and church planter. He taught at the Wayne County Seminary for four years, beginning in 1836. He was a loyal friend and mentor of Lucinda and Oliver P. Morton.*

trustee for the State University at Bloomington, now Indiana University. He became the first President of North Western Christian University (now Butler University). He was State Superintendent of Public Instruction under Governor Morton in 1862, completing the elected term of Miles Fletcher, who had been killed in a railroad accident. Samuel Hoshour was a minister of the Christian Church who had established the Centerville Christian Church and many others. He was as well known throughout Indiana for his church planting and preaching as he was for his excellent qualities as an educator.

Under Professor Hoshour, the cost for the Seminary classes in 1836 ranged from $6 to $9 per class for each school term. The usual cost for local common schools was $1.25 per student per term. He wrote in his autobiography, "It was four years (Wayne County Seminary) under my supervision." He noted that during this time "he had students of the best families of the State of Indiana … such as the two sons of Indiana Governor David Wallace, as well as sons and daughters of professional men, even the son of an Indian Chief." His students also included embryo (in developing stage) judges, governors, and a United States Senator.

During his time at the Seminary, Hoshour mentored some of Centerville and Indiana's outstanding men of the 19th century. Among those men were Indiana Governor and Senator Oliver Morton; General Lew Wallace, son of Governor David Wallace and author of *Ben Hur*; and John Burbank, Governor of the Dakota Territory.

In a letter to Mrs. Lew Wallace after her husband's death, Lucinda Morton wrote of being a classmate of Lew Wallace at the Wayne County Seminary.

*Indianapolis, Feb. 23rd, 1905*

*My Dear Mrs. Wallace,*

*It is with the most profound sorrow that I learn of the death of your beloved husband, Gen. Wallace. I knew him first as a youth in Samuel Hoshour's school in Centerville. He made his home with his aunt, Mrs. Raridan. His cousin Lydia was my most intimate friend and hardly a day passed without meeting him and his brother William.*

*... My sister, Mrs. Gill sends her sympathy to you all.*

*Tearfully and prayerfully, your friend,*

*Lucinda M. Morton*

The letter affirms that Lucinda attended the Seminary with Lew Wallace and at the same time as Oliver Morton. She was educated as well as her brothers. She had excellent preparation to be the wife and companion of such an outstanding intellect and statesman as Oliver P. Morton.

# Chapter 4

# OLIVER HAZARD PERRY THROCK MORTON

Oliver P. Morton, the 14th Governor of Indiana and Lucinda Burbank's future husband, was born August 4, 1823, in Salisbury, the little town that was Wayne County's first county seat. Oliver's father, James Throckmorton, was born in New Jersey in 1782, a descendant of John Throckmorton, who came to America with his friend Roger Williams about 1630. Roger Williams was the founder of the Colony of Rhode Island.

Oliver's father, James Throckmorton, became embittered over the settlement of his father's estate, believing he had been unjustly treated by his brothers. James dropped the surname Throckmorton and changed his name to James Throck Morton (James T. Morton) because he did not want to be associated with the Throckmorton name. He moved to Ohio where he married his first wife, Abigail Bunnell (or Bonnell) in 1806. They had three children, William S., born 1807; Anna Maria, born 1810; and James, born 1812. His son James was killed by a falling tree when about 16 or 17 years old. The other children survived to adulthood.

While living in Ohio, James invested in the Hamilton and Cincinnati Canal, but it did not work out, and he lost most of his money. His next endeavor was innkeeping and then on to becoming a shoemaker.

After his first wife died in 1814, James Morton married Sarah Miller. They moved to Salisbury in the new state of Indiana. Sarah bore him five children, John M., 1815–1819; Ezra and Homer, born 1821, twins who lived only a month; Oliver was born in 1823; and Ephram in 1826, who died in childbirth with his mother. This left Oliver as the only living child of the second marriage. He was three years old when his mother died.

There was no one to care for Oliver so his father sent him to live with his grandparents, John and Hannah Miller, of Springfield, Ohio, and his two widowed aunts. The family was staunch Scotch Presbyterians and strict in their observance of religious training and attending church.

Oliver's two aunts, Hannah Whitaker and Mary (Polly) Whitaker, sisters to his mother, Sarah, cared for the boy. The sisters likely had been married to brothers who were deceased. Another sister, Charlotte Miller, became the first wife of William S. Morton, Oliver's older half brother.

Oliver went to the local school in Ohio where his aunt, Hannah, was the teacher. He read and studied the Bible dutifully and was well acquainted with the Christian faith. Oliver grew to be a healthy boy with a strong work ethic. In his spare time, he read everything he could, including newspapers, sale bills, and books. He was especially fond of books of history and biographies.

Oliver's father was an admirer of Oliver Hazard Perry who was the naval hero of the Battle of Lake Erie in 1813. The battle was a decisive win for the American forces against England in the War of 1812. This admiration for a hero led to Oliver being given the name Oliver Hazard Perry Throck Morton. When Oliver began his law career, his partner suggested that he shorten his name and he began to sign his middle names with initials. He dropped Hazard and Throck for just Oliver Perry Morton. The name Throck was used as a middle name for

Oliver's youngest son and several other Morton family descendants.

Lucinda's father, Isaac Burbank, had met young Oliver on his frequent buying trips to Cincinnati before the boy's family moved to Centerville. Isaac would stop at the Miller farm to stay overnight. The farm was near the town of Old Springfield, Ohio, now Springdale. It was on the Great Road or Springfield Pike, also the stagecoach line, and the main road from Wayne County to Cincinnati. The stagecoach trip took about twelve hours from Centerville to Cincinnati, but much longer for freight wagons or other horse-drawn vehicles. The stagecoach had the right-of-way on the roads to pass the slower traffic. Burbank's trips to Cincinnati would take at least a couple of days to make the purchases and arrange shipping to Centerville.

It was not unusual for farm families to open their homes for travelers to eat meals and stay overnight as paying guests. Travelers could get lodging, meals, feed and water for their horses or oxen, and park their wagons in the barnyard. Young Oliver was an avid reader and saved his money to have Mr. Burbank purchase books for him in Cincinnati. He would pick up whatever books he could find for Oliver and bring them back on his return trip. It was probably not a lucky chance that Burbank stopped at the Miller farm overnight. Oliver's father and older brother were also in business in Centerville and may have suggested the stop at the Miller farm. That would have been convenient for Burbank and he could carry back word of young Oliver to his family.

When Oliver's grandparents and aunts moved to Centerville in 1838, Oliver became close friends with the Burbank sons. Oliver was a year younger than Jacob Edward, Lucinda's older brother. Both boys were schoolmates at the Wayne County Seminary and attended Miami University in Oxford, Ohio at the same time.

Oliver's grandparents and aunts moved so he could attend the Wayne County Seminary and be near his father. Although Oliver was not an outstanding student at the Seminary, he was diligent in his studies. Oliver was tall and strong, and he excelled in athletics and loved to read and debate. He also loved music and was talented in it. After Oliver's grandfather, John Miller, died in late 1838, the expense of the school was too much for the family. At fifteen, his formal schooling ended and he had only attended the Seminary for a year. But the friendships he made there would last a lifetime.

Oliver's father, James Morton, moved from Salisbury to Centerville in 1837, and set up shop as a shoemaker. When Oliver's formal schooling ended, James insisted Oliver begin preparing for a career. Young men were expected to take up useful work at an early age. Oliver went to work for Dr. Swain as a clerk in his apothecary, thinking to study to become a doctor. Oliver and his employer had a falling out over Oliver's habit of reading when he wasn't busy. Their disagreement led to exchanging physical blows and he was fired. This shameful behavior angered his father and as a punishment, he apprenticed Oliver to work for his older half brother, William S. Morton, a hat maker. William was sixteen years older than Oliver and had a good business in Centerville.

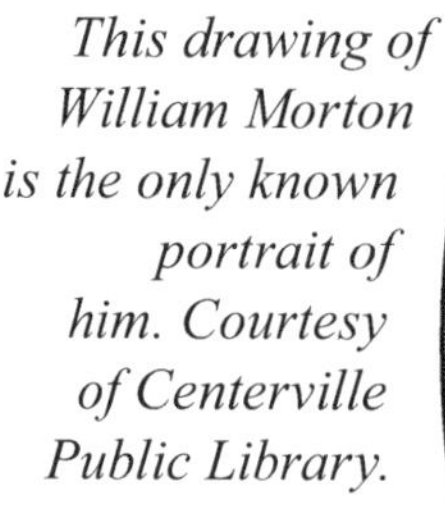

*This drawing of William Morton is the only known portrait of him. Courtesy of Centerville Public Library.*

For nearly four years, Oliver worked for his brother, trying to learn the hatter's trade. Young Oliver felt William was too harsh a taskmaster and he did not want to make hats for a living. Reading and home study were still Oliver's favorite pastimes and he became interested in the law as a career. In 1844, Oliver was able to save

**HATS, HATS.**

**WILLIAM S. T. MORTON,**

RETURNS his sincere thanks to the Citizens of Centreville, and Wayne County, for the very liberal patronage heretofore received, and hopes by giving them good bargains in HATS to merit and receive a continuance of their custom. He has received from New York a very extensive stock of the best FURS and TRIMMINGS, selected by himself, which will enable him to sell HATS on as good terms as any other shop in the West. He invites his old customers and others to call, and he will use his best endeavors to keep them from going home *bare-headed.* His shop is on Main Street, one door East of Delong's Hotel.

☞ The highest price in HATS or CASH will be given for any quantity of *Furs*, and 1,000 pounds of Lambs Wool.

N. B. Those persons who have been indebted to me from one to three years, are respectfully invited to call and pay up, as no longer indulgence can be given.

WILLIAM S. T. MORTON.

Centreville, May 10, 1837. 19–6m.

*Advertisement for William Morton's hats, which appeared in "The Centreville Chronicle" on May 10, 1837.*

enough money to pay his brother to get out of the remainder of his apprenticeship.

Oliver had received an inheritance from his grandfather Miller and with this and the money he saved, he decided to get more education. His plan was to go to Miami University in Oxford, Ohio. Although Oliver did not graduate from any school, he was educated enough to pass the entrance exam at the university. Oliver's years at Miami University helped him gain confidence. He was a good student, taking the courses that he felt would help him in a law career. When he wasn't busy with his studies, he was an excellent athlete, loved debating, and enjoyed musical activities. Even with scrimping and saving, two years was all Oliver could afford.

At the end of Oliver's first year at Miami, Lucinda Burbank went with a party of girls to attend the graduation ceremony at the university, probably for her brother. Even though Oliver was acquainted with the younger sister of his good friend Jacob Burbank, he now saw her as a lovely young lady and fell in love with her. After his second year at the university, Oliver left to take up the study of law and get married.

# Chapter 5

# LAW AND MARRIAGE

Lucinda Burbank and Oliver Morton married on May 15, 1845. He was 22 and she was 20. Their good friend, spiritual advisor, and mentor Samuel Hoshour, married them at the Burbank home, the apartment above the Burbank Mercantile. The wedding took place in the front double parlors that could be opened into one large room. The building is still in use at 113 E. Main Street in Centerville. In 1969, the roof of the building was damaged in a fire. It was rebuilt and the upper floor and roofline were changed.

There are no pictures of Lucinda and Oliver in their early years of marriage. However, William Dudley Foulke, Oliver P. Morton's first biographer, described Lucinda. He had known her personally for several years and consulted her while writing his book. According to Foulke, she was "a woman of quiet, retiring manners, practical, affectionate, entirely devoted to him and to their children."

Oliver was described as tall, "large and sturdy," with black hair and dark eyes. He was outgoing and made friends easily. Morton was described in his youth as having a winning smile and was persuasive in his ways.

At the time of her marriage, Lucinda was well prepared to become a wife and mother. She loved to read books and followed the current

State of Indiana

Original

**Marriage Certificate**

I, Samuel K. Hoshour, hereby certify that on the 15 day of May, one thousand eight hundred and 45 at Centreville in the County of Wayne, State of Indiana, Groom Oliver P.H. Morton of Wayne County, State of Indiana,

and

Bride Maria Lucinda Burbank of Wayne County, State of Indiana, were by me united in

**Marriage**

as authorized by a marriage license issued for that purpose by the Clerk of the Circuit Court of Wayne County, and State of Indiana, dated the 15 day of May 1845

Signed Thos. G. Noble

Official Designation Clk

Wayne Circuit Court

Centreville, Ind.

*Marriage certificate for Oliver and Lucinda Morton. Signed by Samuel Hoshour, May 18, 1845. From the Historic Mansion House collection.*

events that came in newspapers and magazines. She was raised observing her father's prosperous mercantile business and it is likely that she had helped out in the store. She would have learned about wholesale costs and how to select the best products for the customers. This knowledge would help her manage her household money and to be frugal through the hard years of the Civil War.

Lucinda was a woman of her time, learning homemaking skills at her mother's knee. She, her mother, and sisters shared the work of caring for a family of nine, while the brothers helped their father with the store. Lucinda learned to prepare meals, to become proficient in all kinds of needlework and sewing, and to do whatever was necessary to care for the home and family. There were few conveniences available to aid the housewife while Lucinda grew up. Difficult jobs around the house had to be done frequently, such as washing and ironing the clothes, preparing food from scratch, and cleaning. Many housewives of the 1830s and 1840s still made most of their family's clothing. New improvements came in the 1850s, with cook stoves replacing fireplace cooking, sewing machines, and clothes wringers for washtubs. Spinning wheels and looms were still used in many homes to spin thread and to weave cloth. When she was married, Lucinda was ready to care for her household and to entertain guests. Oliver turned over the care of their home and most of their finances to her.

Lucinda and her siblings had been prominent in Centerville social circles. There were church socials, school events, skating and sledding parties in the winter, picnics and parties in the summer. The Courthouse, with its large auditorium, was a popular place for political and religious speakers and other entertainment. Families and friends often visited in each other's homes. Out-of-town visitors might stay overnight or for several days. Lucinda's family was well acquainted with their neighbors and was respected in the Centerville community. There was little that went on in Centerville that was not common knowledge. Lucinda and Oliver, no doubt, had crossed each other's paths many times, both having attended the Seminary and living in close proximity of each other in the busy little town.

The Burbank family was fond of Oliver, and no doubt, helped the young couple to get started. The family offered strong support to them as shown through the war years when her sisters helped Lucinda in Indianapolis and when her sons needed to stay in Centerville. The Burbank grandparents or other family members kept the boys when they attended school at the Seminary. Loving care from the extended family helped sustain Lucinda at the time of Oliver's last illness and death.

Oliver began his study of law in 1845, in the office of John Newman, a leading attorney in Centerville. Newman had become an important influence in the state, having been elected as a representative to the State Legislature in 1834. In 1847, he was chosen the President of the Whitewater Valley Canal Company, serving for five years. In 1851, he became President of the Indiana Central Railway Company, the company that built the railroad from Indianapolis to Richmond. Newman's connections with these new forms of investments and transportation opened important doors for Oliver's law career.

There was little formal law training available in Indiana for law students, and most began their careers as an apprentice or clerk in a law office. Oliver was diligent in his studies and soon became Newman's junior partner. He was described by Newman as "laborious in his studies, strictly temperate in his habits, and genial in his manners." Oliver had learned to be thorough in his reading and "possessed a remarkable degree in the power of thinking at all times and in every place." In other words, he was a powerful speaker and debater in the courtroom.

After Oliver had settled into his new career, he became a member of the Dark Lyceum of Centerville. The debating society was started by George W. Julian to help him overcome shyness and timidity. Julian and a friend began debating, each one taking a side as lawyers do in arguing a case. Julian was three years older than Oliver, and over the years, they became bitter enemies, even though they came from the same town, debated together, and were associated with the same political party. The Dark Lyceum usually met in the Seminary building. It was called "Dark" Lyceum because the young lawyers debated in darkness so that they could overcome their timidity when arguing the evening's topic. Other young lawyers soon asked to join the society and the debates became a popular form of entertainment in town.

Oliver stayed with the firm of Newman and Test until 1849, when he decided to set up his own law practice. In a few months, he brought in a junior partner, Nimrod Johnson. This partnership continued until 1852.

*Advertisement for*
*Oliver P. Morton's law office.*
*"The Jeffersonian," 1848.*

# Chapter 6

# THE YOUNG FAMILY

Oliver and Lucinda started their family with the birth of their first son, John M., in 1846. Two baby daughters were born but lived only a short time. Mary Elizabeth was born in 1848 and died in 1849, and Sarah Lilas was born in 1850 and died in 1852. Lucinda had lost both of her little daughters, and although it was not unusual for babies not to survive in those days, the pain of a child's death always causes grief for the parents. No doubt, Lucinda's mother was a tower of strength to her daughter, because she, too, had lost two babies.

Oliver had been practicing law for about seven years and had served a short term as a judge of the Court of Common Pleas. His law practice was thriving, but having served as a judge, he recognized his need for more training and education in the law.

The winter term of six months at the Cincinnati Law School began in January 1853. With Lucinda's understanding and blessing, Oliver knew that her family was close and supportive, so he was able to stay in Cincinnati to study.

Oliver's grandmother, Hannah Miller, passed away in 1846, the same year as Lucinda gave birth to their first son, John. His aunt, Hannah Whitaker, died in 1850 and aunt, Mary (Polly) Whitaker, died in 1851. Another aunt and sister of his mother, Charlotte Morton, also died in 1851. Charlotte was the first wife of Oliver's older brother, William Morton. The Miller and Morton families had been intertwined since James, Oliver's father, married Sarah Miller, and Oliver's half brother William married her sister. The deaths of all the Miller women grieved James Morton and his sons, William and Oliver.

Lucinda and Oliver had set up housekeeping after they were married in his aunts' family home. Oliver had moved with his grandmother and his two aunts to 115 S. Cross (Morton) Street. Oliver inherited

*Oliver's home at 115 South Cross (Morton) Street.*

half of the house when his aunt, Hannah died, and he inherited the other half from the estate of his aunt, Mary. Oliver and Lucinda lived in this house until they purchased the Jacob Julian home at 319 West Main Street.

Upon returning to Centerville after his term of study in Cincinnati, Oliver formed a new partnership with John F. Kibbey. Oliver loved to talk and debate with his fellow lawyers. He was a member of the local I.O.O.F. Lodge. During this time with Kibbey, his office kept an open door that welcomed young lawyers to come by to ask questions and discuss legal matters. Kibbey oversaw a library of law books that was available for the young lawyers to borrow. The firm of Morton & Kibbey prospered, and Oliver's income grew along with his law practice.

The new communication system of the telegraph began operating through Wayne County in 1849. The Indiana Central Railroad came through Centerville in 1853. Oliver's law office handled many legal matters for the new railroad that paid him very well. His reputation as a brilliant lawyer brought in clients from surrounding counties, Indianapolis, and western Ohio. This time of a lucrative private practice was the basis of Oliver's wealth.

Law business in Centerville continued to grow, and there were many opportunities for lawyers. Some of early Indiana's most influential lawyers lived in Centerville. The Morton & Kibbey law practice was second in prominence only to John Newman's firm.

In 1856, Lucinda's fourth child, Walter Scott, was born. With the steady increase in income, Oliver and Lucinda were able to purchase a large, fine brick home in December 1857, for $5,000. The house was built by Judge Jacob Julian in 1847–1848. The house still stands at the west edge of Centerville, 319 West Main Street.

*The Morton's home at 319 West Main Street. The house was added to the National Register of Historic Places in 1975. Courtesy of Historic Centerville.*

Centerville of the 1840s–1860s was a bustling county seat town where the political business and the courts of Wayne County were conducted. Large numbers of people were moving west on the National Road. There were several hotels and taverns available for overnight visitors. The Western Stage line stopped at the Mansion

*Historic Mansion House located at 319 East Main Street in Centerville. This was a hotel and stagecoach stop for many years. The old Salisbury Courthouse was moved to this property in the early 1970s. From the author's collection.*

House hotel and was a source of news coming from other parts of the country. Preachers, politicians, salesmen, entertainers, and assorted businessmen regularly came on the stagecoach to Centerville. When the railroad came through, much of the stagecoach business was lost. Several newspapers were printed there at various times, printing mostly political, regional, and national news. They were also full of advertisements for the various business opportunities.

Hundreds of people, wagons, and horses continued to travel the Cumberland–National Road through Centerville, heading west.

During the weekdays and Saturday, the town was noisy and crowded. Covered wagons, freight wagons, and all kinds of carriages rumbled through. Horses, oxen, and groups of cattle, sheep, or hogs clopped their hooves against the stone paving. The droppings of their dung made the town smell of the animals. It took a lot of work to keep the main streets cleaned up of refuse. The town was noisy with dogs, caged chickens, and penned domestic animals, as well as everything coming through town. In 1853, a new source of noise, dirt, and smoke was added by the coming of at least two trains a day, with loud whistles and bells. The black smoke from the locomotives and the smoke from cooking and heating fires carried dirt all over the town.

*Wagon train moving west. Multitudes of horses, wagons, carriages, and stagecoaches passed through Centerville on the National Road.*

But on Sundays, things quieted down. No business was allowed on Sundays, so the stores were closed and it was worship time at the churches. The church bells rang out calling to the worshipers. Church services were held morning and evening. Sunday was an important day of rest for the people.

Centerville had its own class of "best families," whose social life was equal to many larger cities of Indiana. In her new house, Lucinda was able to practice gracious hospitality for her family and friends as well as entertaining her husband's expanding political acquaintances. Oliver's busy life and his growing political interests brought many guests to their home.

Centerville native Anna Lashley, Morton's neighbor, who was a young girl at the time, was interviewed in 1919.

"The (Oliver) Mortons were among the most honored citizens of the town who often gave parties and " hops" (dance parties) in their home. Many a time as a girl, I went dancing through their spacious rooms and walked around the lawn in the moonlight." Anna recalled. The parties were for friends, and no strong drinks were served at the Morton home, as they agreed with the temperance movement.

# Chapter 7

## POLITICS

Oliver left the home care to Lucinda and trusted her with money matters. Oliver was a hard worker, putting in long hours at his office. He enjoyed spending time with friends, discussing current affairs and politics. Lucinda became accustomed to Oliver's long hours at his job, but they still found time to enjoy social activities. Morton's office was a few blocks from his house, and he could walk home for meals if he chose.

Oliver took time from his law practice to be involved in county and state politics. He relied on his partner, John Kibbey, to handle affairs at the office. Kibbey took care of office details, and Oliver concentrated on his speeches and court cases. His first attempt at being elected was in 1848, when he ran for the district office of prosecuting attorney. The district covered several counties that were primarily of the Whig Party. Oliver was a young lawyer, relatively unknown at the time and a Democrat, so his chances of winning were slim and he was defeated.

Social issues and politics filled the local and state newspapers. Along with Indiana's financial crisis of the 1830s, over the fiasco of internal improvements, the topics of slavery and temperance received a lot of press. The several newspapers in Wayne County had strong political views and strongly challenged those who disagreed with them. Between the talk around town, and political and religious speakers regularly giving speeches in Centerville and Richmond, there was hardly any way to be ignorant of what was going on.

Lucinda could not help but be aware of the issues with Oliver's law cases and speeches, since they were often in the news. Lucinda's father and brothers took part in local politics, and when her brothers moved west to Nebraska in the late 1850s, they took part in politics there. According to Morton's biographer, William Dudley Foulke, Oliver respected Lucinda's opinion and he read his speeches to her before he gave them.

The Democratic Party and Oliver bitterly parted ways in 1854. The divisive issue of the expansion of slavery into new territories caused Oliver to strongly disagree with his party. The Kansas–Nebraska Act, backed by the Democrats, would allow each territory or state to decide whether they would allow slavery. This would violate the Missouri Compromise of 1820 that had kept slave states from becoming too powerful. A new state coming into the Union that encouraged slavery was balanced with a state that did not allow slavery.

Wayne County was known for its anti-slave politics. The many people who settled in the Richmond and Centerville area were of the Friends or Quaker faith. Most had deliberately moved from slave states to free states so they would not have to tolerate anyone owning slaves, nor see how badly they were treated. Quakers supported the complete abolition of slavery.

Levi Coffin, sometimes referred to as "the President of the Underground Railroad," came to Indiana in 1826. He was a Quaker, abolitionist, businessman, and humanitarian. He opened a dry goods store in Newport, now the town of Fountain City, a few miles north of Richmond. He and his wife opened their home to become a place of refuge for escaping slaves on the Underground Railroad. He also helped organize the Newport Temperance Society and worked to remove liquor from being sold in Newport and Wayne County. Centerville passed an ordinance against liquor in 1843. But even with the strong feeling against liquor, it was never completely eradicated

*The Levi Coffin House in Fountain City, Indiana is now an Indiana State Historic Site. In 1966, the home became the first property in the state to be added to the National Register of Historic Places, and it is also a National Historic Landmark. The Coffins built the house in 1837.*

throughout the county or state. Coffin did business in Centerville and had many friends and business associates there. The Levi Coffin house in Fountain City is owned by the State of Indiana and is a historic house museum.

The Women's Rights movement was coming to the forefront as a social issue in Indiana. It was debated in the newspapers, but most politicians did not give it much attention. The first Women's Rights convention in Indiana was held in Dublin, a village about seventeen miles west of Richmond, on the National Road. Supporters gathered at the Dublin Friends Meeting on October 14–15, 1851. The convention adopted resolutions for political, social, and financial rights for women. Both women and men attended the meeting. They supported the abolition of slaves, temperance, and women's suffrage. Several of the surrounding counties sent representatives to the meeting, and the majority of them were Quakers. The local newspapers had much to comment upon, both pro and con.

Lucinda was well informed of local news through Oliver's work and her family's store in the heart of town. After the Women's Rights convention, there was more talk about it. Mrs. Henrietta Rose, the wife of a Centerville doctor, wrote a novel titled *Nora Wilmot: A Tale of Temperance and Woman's Rights,* published in 1858. The Victorian romantic love story is about how a man's drunken behavior ruined his family. Included in the book is the fictional description of a Women's Rights convention. It is likely that the author had attended the convention in Dublin. The novel's characters traveled on the train, a relatively new transportation in the area. The Indiana Central Railroad had not been finished at the time of the Women's Rights meeting, but by the time Mrs. Rose wrote her book, it connected Richmond, Centerville, Cambridge City, and Dublin with daily trains.

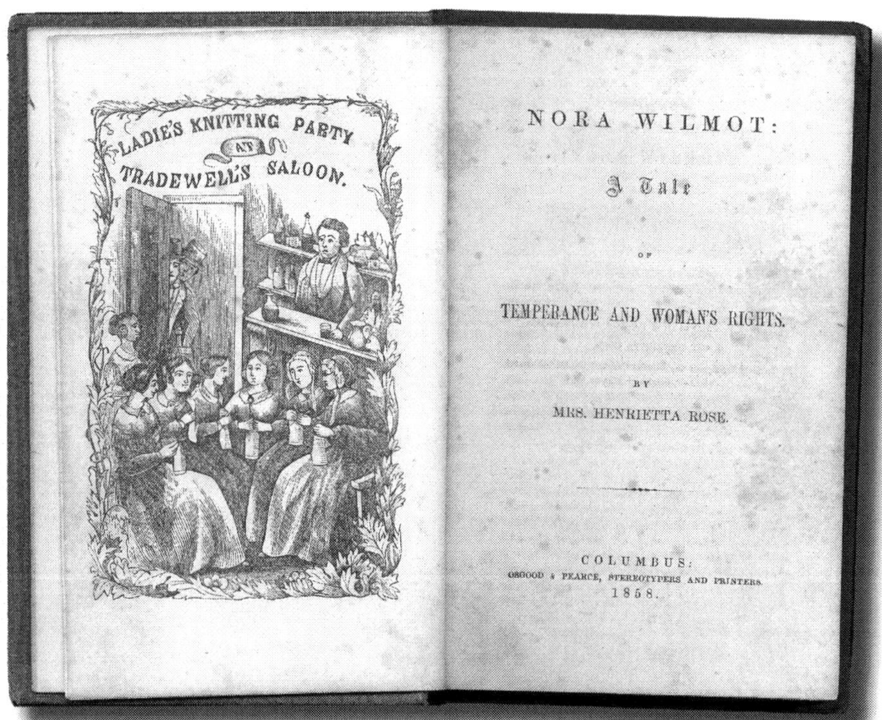


*An 1858 novel by Henrietta Rose, "Nora Wilmot: A Tale of Temperance and Woman's Rights." Image courtesy of Between the Covers Rare Books, Inc., New Jersey.*

Mrs. Rose's book presents light on the local attitudes of Centerville and surrounding communities concerning the three dominant social issues of abolition of slavery, temperance, and women's rights. Many years later, Mrs. Rose's book is given credit for writing the first women's rights novel. Women's rights became an important issue to support for Senator Morton and for Lucinda and her son, Oliver T.

After leaving the Democrat Party, Oliver looked for other political groups that were more in agreement with his ideas. Men of like mind across the country were seeking to form a new party and Oliver helped organize the Republican Party in 1854. He had been a loyal Democrat but was becoming more involved with the issue of slavery. While Oliver was not actively anti-slavery and was mistrustful of abolitionists, he was against slavery spreading to new states in the west.

Politics became increasingly important to Oliver, and he often traveled around the county and state making political speeches. Oliver ran for Indiana governor in 1856, on the newly formed Republican Party ticket. His schedule of speeches would have exhausted a less strong man. From July 10 to October 13, 1856, he gave fifty-six speeches throughout Indiana. This much travel would not have been possible without the trains. Other transportation would have been horseback, buggy, or stagecoaches that were still in use where there were no trains. Often his speeches, debates with the opposing candidate, and other meetings started at 1:00 p.m. in the afternoon and lasted until evening. Several times, he gave speeches for seven days straight, with only a couple of days off before traveling again. Oliver could not always come home after the meetings. Lucinda took care of things at home and his law partner saw to their office. Even with all this exhaustive effort, Oliver lost his bid for governor.

Lucinda's fifth child, Oliver Throck, was born in 1860. For a short time, Oliver had been discouraged about his political ambitions but soon regained his political enthusiasm. The election for governor of Indiana was underway, and Oliver began his campaign for

Lieutenant Governor, with Henry Lane for Governor. They ran a successful campaign and Lane was elected Governor and Morton as Lieutenant Governor of Indiana. After only two days in office, Lane resigned and was appointed to the U.S. Senate. Morton replaced Lane as Governor and was inaugurated on January 16, 1861, in a move that apparently was calculated before the election.

Before Oliver was able to relocate to Indianapolis and take over his new job, he and Lucinda had a warning of what might be coming to threaten them. After his election, on a Friday night in late November 1860, Oliver was returning from Richmond to Centerville. When his buggy was opposite Earlham College, someone tried to stop his horse by seizing it by the bridle. According to the Richmond newspaper, "The horse became frightened and suddenly wheeling around and nearly upsetting the buggy, he put back for town on a run. Mr. M, (Morton) altho' 'twas quite dark, distinctly saw the figure of a man, and supposing there might be a gang of them, he prudently concluded to stay all night at his brother-in-law's."

The newspaper continues, "Evidently disappointed at not

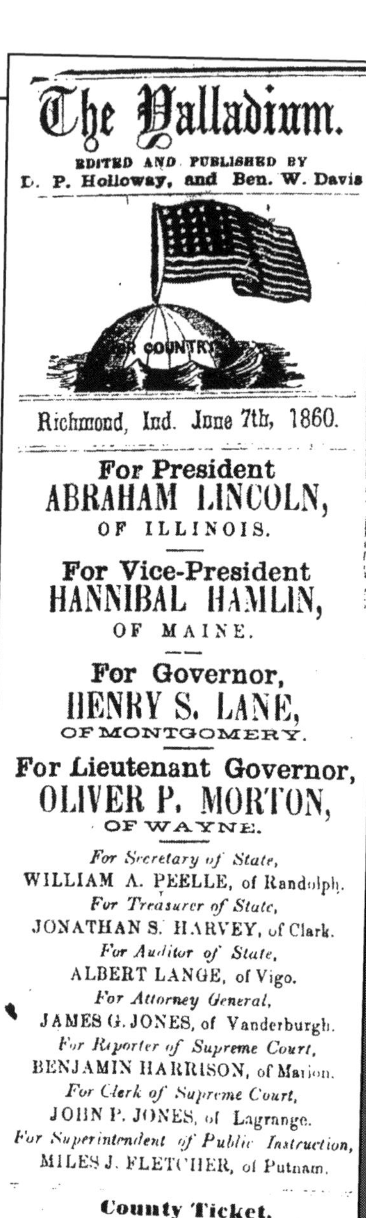

The Palladium.

EDITED AND PUBLISHED BY
D. P. Holloway, and Ben. W. Davis

Richmond, Ind. June 7th, 1860.

For President
ABRAHAM LINCOLN,
OF ILLINOIS.

For Vice-President
HANNIBAL HAMLIN,
OF MAINE.

For Governor,
HENRY S. LANE,
OF MONTGOMERY.

For Lieutenant Governor,
OLIVER P. MORTON,
OF WAYNE.

For Secretary of State,
WILLIAM A. PEELLE, of Randolph.
For Treasurer of State,
JONATHAN S. HARVEY, of Clark.
For Auditor of State,
ALBERT LANGE, of Vigo.
For Attorney General,
JAMES G. JONES, of Vanderburgh.
For Reporter of Supreme Court,
BENJAMIN HARRISON, of Marion.
For Clerk of Supreme Court,
JOHN P. JONES, of Lagrange.
For Superintendent of Public Instruction,
MILES J. FLETCHER, of Putnam.

County Ticket.
For Common Pleas Judge
JERRE M. WILSON.
For Prosecuting Attorney
JOHN C. WHITRIDGE.
Representatives.
E. B. NEWMAN, OLIVER T. JONES,
ISRAEL WOODRUFF.
Treasurer—C. B. HUFF.
Sheriff—JOS. S. STEDHAM.
Surveyor—ROBERT C. SHUTE.
Commissioner—JONATHAN BALDWIN.
Coroner—JESSE STEVENS.

*National Republican Election ticket, 1860. From the "Indianapolis Journal."*

making a "haul" from Judge M., the gang of thieves attempted to enter the residence of Stephen C. Mendenhall, thro' one of the back windows. The noise made in raising it attracted the attention of our old friend Bonner, who seized an old shooting-iron, but before he could 'draw a beed' on the scamps, they heard him making preparations to give them a warm reception, and they speedily decamped."

From the time Oliver P. Morton served as a judge, he was called Judge Morton until he was Governor Morton. From this time on, he was either called Governor Morton, Senator Morton, or just plain Morton, when mentioned in newspapers, books, and articles.

He was not deterred by the threat and prepared to move into the Governor's office. Morton and Lucinda were quickly engaged in the roiling events leading up to the Civil War.

# Part 2

# MRS. GOVERNOR MORTON

# Chapter 8

# THE GOVERNOR'S HOUSE

The first order of business for Lucinda as the wife of Indiana's new Governor was making the move from Centerville to the capital. The local newspaper reported on January 24, 1861 that the Mortons had moved to Indianapolis. They had lived in their fine brick house in Centerville for less than four years. They did not sell it in case they might move back after his term of Governor was over. As Lucinda prepared to move, she may have heard stories about the first Governor's Mansion and the one currently in use.

Before the Indiana capital was moved from Corydon to Indianapolis in 1821, Alexander Ralston and Elias Fordham were commissioned to make a plan for the new city of Indianapolis. The city map was drawn with a circle at its center, designated "Circle Street," in the middle of the mile square plat. It was located in the center of Indianapolis where four streets intersected—North and South Meridian Streets and East and West Market Streets. The main street was Washington Street (a part of the National Road), located one block south of the Circle. It ran east and west through the city.

After the State House was built, it was decided that the governor should have an official residence in Indianapolis. The Indiana legislature voted to spend $4,000 to build a house and put it in a suitable location. Ralston suggested that the residence should be near the city

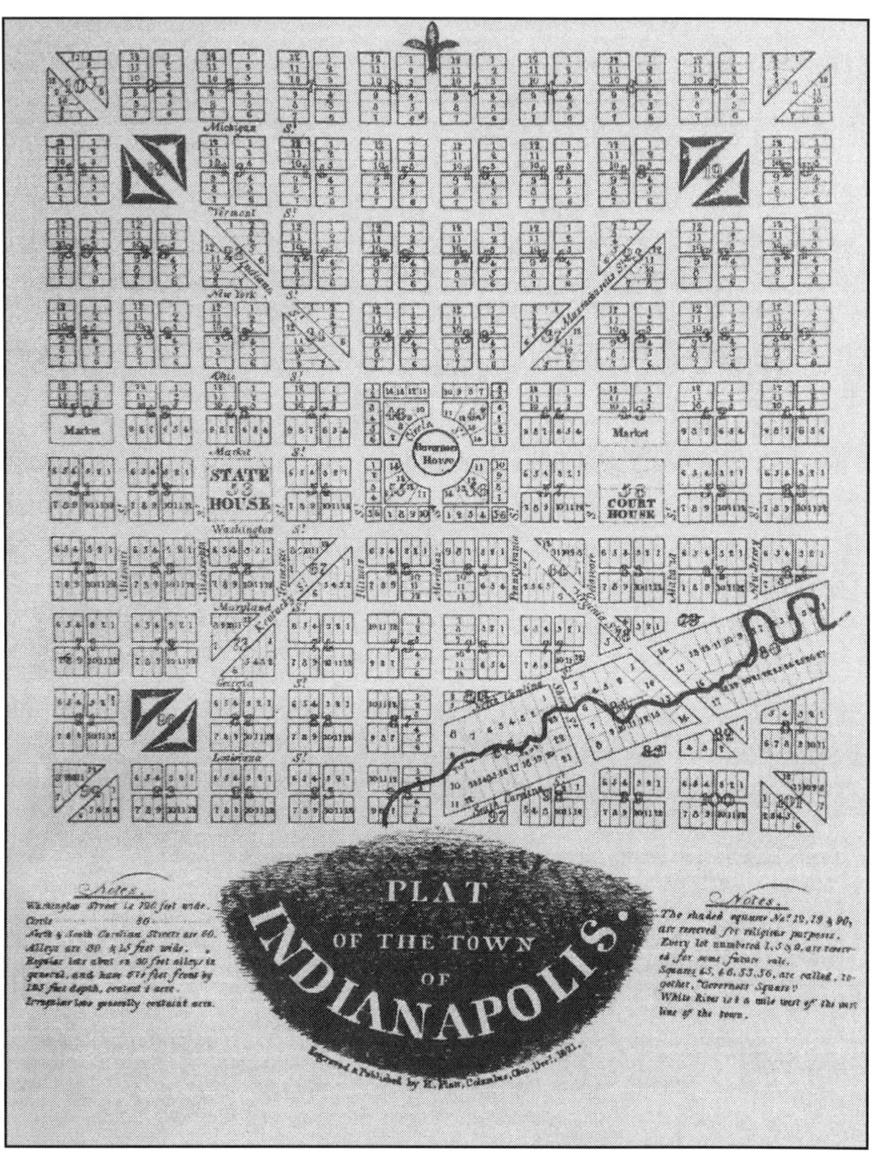


*An 1821 plat of Indianapolis. Courtesy of Indiana Historical Society.*

center, placing it on the Circle where the Indiana State Soldiers' and Sailors' Monument now stands. The four central blocks surrounding it were called the Governor's Square. The house was completed in 1829, costing $6,500. The house faced south, with two stories, an attic, and basement, and was made of yellow brick. It was six feet off the ground with an impressive staircase leading to the front door.

John Parsons continued to Indianapolis after his visit to Centerville in 1840, and he visited the old Governor's House on his tour of Indianapolis. "It was with considerable curiosity that I approached the 'Mansion,' which until now I had viewed only from afar. This location in the center of the Circle was chosen, I was told, because it is central and lies away from the main business street with its disturbing uproar and constant crowd of passengers. The Circle is enclosed in a neat rail fence; the house is large and square, two full stories with a low, slightly inclined roof covering an attic story, lighted by a dormer window on each of the four sides. On the roof there was a 'flat' about twelve feet square, surrounded by a balustrade (railing), intended for a resort in the cool of the evening, for the family to sit and overlook the city on summer evenings."

Parsons' description continued, "The floor of the first story is

*The house was built on the Circle in Indianapolis as the Governor's Mansion, but was never lived in by a governor.*

raised some four feet or so above the ground, and is reached by a broad flight of steps at each side. It is divided off from north to south and east to west by two wide halls crossing at right angles, making a large room in each of the four corners, and the partitions on this floor are made with sliding panels, so that they can be thrown into one room on the occasion of a ball or levee (reception for an important person)."

Although the new "mansion" appeared to be a fine house, First Lady Esther Ray, wife of Governor James Ray, 1825–1831, would not move into it and declared it was unsuitable for a family. Without suggestions from Mrs. Ray to the builders, it was designed with no kitchen, pantry, or closets. In addition, there would be little privacy because it stood in such a prominent place. According to Mrs. Ray, "... every family in town would be able to inspect my washing on Monday morning."

In order to encourage Mrs. Ray to change her mind, she was reminded that two lots across from the Circle had been purchased for use by the Governor's family. One of the lots was for a yard and garden. The other lot was for a stable and land for the Governor's horse and carriage. But Mrs. Ray flatly refused to move into the house. She felt it was not arranged to suit family living. The house was drafty and the basement damp. With Mrs. Ray's refusal to use it, the following governors' families also refused, and the house was never occupied by a governor's family. A stipend of $200 per year was given to compensate for not having a place suitable for the Governor's family. The Rays lived with their five children in the beautiful home they had built at the corner of Madison Street and Ohio Street.

Not knowing what to do with the building built for the Governor, it was turned over to the state officials who used the main floor for offices and court space. The first-floor rooms could be opened and were used for any social occasions desired by the Governor. The State Library was housed there until 1841, when it was moved to the State House. The judges of the Supreme Court and others used the second-floor rooms. By the 1850s, the building had fallen into disrepair and the legislature of 1856–1857 ordered it to be sold. It was auctioned in April 1857, and torn down.

Governor David Wallace, father of General Lew Wallace, was elected as Governor in 1837. There was still a need for a Governor's House. An allowance of $500 was paid for the Wallace family to rent a house at the corner of Washington Street and Missouri Street.

In January 1839, the residence of Dr. John H. Sanders was offered for sale. The house was on the northwest corner of Illinois Street and West Market Street, just a short walk from the State House. The sale description stated that the house was eighty by thirty-two feet, with six rooms on the first floor and five rooms on the second floor. The advertisement suggested that the "five above stairs so arranged as to provide for entertaining 200 to 300 persons," which meant that the upstairs was arranged to throw open doors to make one large room. Dr. Sanders' reason for selling was that he was planning "to go west." At the time, it was considered the finest residence in the city. Governor Wallace's family was the first to live in the new Governor's House.

Henry S. Lane won the election of 1860, but served only two days as Governor, when he resigned to become a U.S. Senator. Oliver P. Morton, elected as Lieutenant Governor, became the Governor and was inaugurated on January 16, 1861, as the 14th Governor of Indiana. It had been prearranged for Lane to move to the U.S. Senate if he should win the election and Morton to become the Governor.

Lucinda and Oliver Morton moved to Indianapolis with their young family. Their son John was fifteen, Walter was five, and baby Oliver T. about eight months old. They had heard about the Governor's residence and were not surprised that they could not move in immediately.

The Governor's House on Market Street and Illinois Street did not seem like a very desirable place to move into, especially as three First Ladies and a Governor had died during the time they lived in it.

Some of their deaths were blamed on the poor condition of the house. But the house was the official residence for Indiana's Governor, so the Morton family moved in.

*The Governor's House at the corner of Market Street and Illinois Street.*

The house was damp, cold, drafty, and in disrepair. A few years earlier, when the street in front of the house was improved, it caused a run-off of water to come into the basement.

The house had been the Governor's residence for 21 years when Lucinda and Morton took possession of it. It needed quite a bit of work and the State Legislature passed an appropriation to pay for new wallpaper and painting. It took a few weeks before the work was finished. Although the house had nine rooms and was two stories tall, it was not large enough for the amount of entertaining and overnight guests that came to it. In order to add more space, Lucinda asked Oliver to build on another room, which he did at their own expense.

In 1896, Lucinda was interviewed about her war memories for *The Indiana Woman* magazine. She described the Governor's Mansion and some of the events that occurred there.

"The Governor's House set back from Market Street a short distance, on the spot, as nearly as I remember, where the Cyclorama building now stands."

The Cyclorama was a large, round, domed building in front of the State House. Its location was about a block south and west of the Governor's House. From 1888–1890, it held a huge 360-degree mural of the Civil War Battle of Atlanta. The novelty of it soon wore off and the mural was sold and the building torn down. The Interurban Traction Terminal was built there. It was the major electric train station in Indianapolis and the largest in the world. It operated from 1904–1941. The present-day Indianapolis Hilton Hotel is located there at 120 West Market Street. The Governor's House was on the north side of Market Street, with the front facing south.

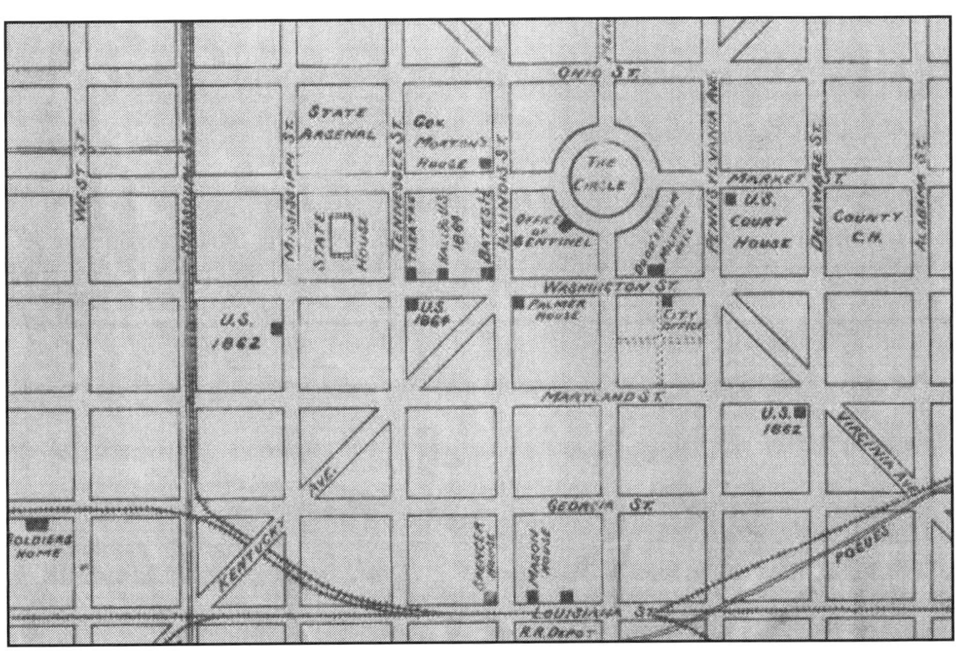


*This Civil War era map shows the Circle, the Stats House, Governor Morton's House, the State Arsenal, the Soldiers' Home, Bates House Hotel, the Railroad Depot, and Pogue's Run. Courtesy of Indiana State Library.*

Lucinda continued, "It was a two-story brick house with Colonial doors and a long hall extending the length of the house. There were double parlors to the left of the hall, both rather commodious rooms. The dining room and kitchen were located at the north end of the house. The upper story was over the double parlors and the remainder but one story."

Lucinda described a long porch and the large yard with several cherry trees and grapevines. The new room was built at the front of the porch. The extra room gave some relief for the crowding, but she always felt there was never enough space for all the visitors and guests. It was in this house that many political and social functions were held. Whenever there were visiting dignitaries to the city, and it was often during the Civil War, they were entertained and sometimes stayed in the house overnight.

There was only a limited budget to work with. The annual salary for the Governor was only $1,500 in 1861. Former Governor Wright had addressed this in 1857, in his last address to the Assembly of the Indiana Legislature. He urged an increase in the salary, saying it was not possible to do all the things necessary unless the Governor had a private income. Wright himself gave up lucrative earning opportunities, and instead, dedicated himself to serve the public as governor. Ashbel P. Willard, the next governor, also made the plea for more salary before he died in October 1860.

## President Lincoln's Visit

Lucinda had barely settled in the house and become used to the demands of being the wife of the Governor of Indiana, when Abraham Lincoln came to visit. On Monday, February 11, 1861, the newly elected President Lincoln came to Indianapolis while on his way to the inauguration in Washington, D.C. He boarded a special early morning train in Springfield, Illinois with a small party of associates. The day was warm, bright, and pleasant for February. The special train made three stops in Illinois. The first stop in Indiana was at the small town of State Line City, where the President-elect made a short speech. A large enthusiastic crowd had gathered, waving flags and handkerchiefs. The booming of a cannon accompanied the train as it departed.

The next stop was at Attica, where cheering crowds met the train. Lincoln made stops and short speeches in Lafayette, Thorntown,

Lebanon, and Zionsville. His train was expected in Indianapolis at 5:00. Preparations had begun early in the day as flags and bunting were hung from every public building and many businesses. Decorations lined the streets from the depot to the Bates House Hotel.

*An 1860 photograph of Abraham Lincoln taken by Matthew Brady.*

The noon trains arriving at the depot brought hundreds of passengers to witness the arrival and reception of President Lincoln.

Both houses of the Indiana Legislature met briefly in the afternoon, until 4:00 when they adjourned. A committee of legislators had left on Saturday to meet the train at State Line City. They welcomed Lincoln and accompanied him to Indianapolis.

Military companies, bands, and fire companies assembled in Indianapolis for the parade. People lined up along Washington Street for the best places to see the President. A lookout had been stationed on the dome of the State House and just before 5:00, when the train came in sight, he waved his hat and the thunder of thirty-four guns fired by the City Grey's Artillery saluted the train as it pulled into Union Depot. It stopped at the intersection of the Lafayette Railroad and Washington Street. A huge, enthusiastic, and cheering crowd of Hoosiers waved flags and handkerchiefs, anxiously waiting to hear from President Lincoln. According to an account by John Hay, Lincoln's secretary, who accompanied him, "Apparently the entire population of Indianapolis and the surrounding territory were in attendance and its enthusiasm at fever heat."

Governor Morton and Lincoln met on the rear platform of the train. Morton greeted him with these words, "Sir: On behalf of the people of Indiana, I bid you welcome. They avail themselves of this occasion to offer their tribute of high respect to your character, as a man and as a statesman, and in your person to honor the high office to which you have been elected." He continued his speech of welcome for several minutes.

Lincoln greeted Morton and the crowd and spoke of his appreciation for having grown up in Indiana. His address was short, and he told the crowd he was not prepared to make a lengthy speech until he arrived in Washington. Morton and Lincoln left the train and were driven to the Bates House Hotel in a luxurious, open carriage drawn by four white horses, finely decorated. They were accompanied by four uniformed military companies, two bands, and three steam fire engines, tenders, and hose carriages. Several other carriages held dignitaries, including Officers of the General Assembly and of the State, Judges of the Supreme Court, and City Council members. Hundreds of people followed behind them. Washington Street was 120 feet wide and so jammed full of people that the procession hardly had room to get through. The houses along the route were decorated and their windows and doors were filled with spectators.

Throngs of people surrounded the Bates House Hotel where Lincoln was staying and wanted to hear more from him. He came out on a second-story balcony to address them. His speech lasted for twenty minutes. Lincoln thanked his listeners for their magnificent welcome and touched on national matters, briefly addressing the situation of the seceding states and the possibility of military action. Some of his remarks and encouraging words were humorous, bringing out shouts of laughter. According to *The Evansville Daily Journal*, "The hearty greeting and responses of the people show that they have entire confidence in his management of the Government." The large

*The Bates House Hotel. Abraham Lincoln spoke from a balcony of this hotel.*

gathering then called for Governor Morton, and he addressed the people with a short speech.

The crowd finally dispersed and after an evening meal for Lincoln's party, a formal reception was held. At 7:30 p.m., members of the Legislature were introduced to the President in the drawing rooms of the Bates House Hotel. The rooms were opened at 8:00 to the ladies and other gentlemen who were attending. As the wife of the Governor, Lucinda would have joined her husband as reception hosts. Lincoln continued meeting people and shaking hands to a late hour. His party retired for the night at the hotel.

The next day was Lincoln's birthday, February 12, 1861. He was fifty-two years old. Early in the morning, Lincoln and his companions walked the short distance from the hotel to the Governor's Mansion, where they were served breakfast. Lucinda gave an account of it in 1896.

"In those days we didn't have breakfast at 12 o'clock as now, but about 9 o'clock and not later than 10 at the outside. The table was set in the form of an 'L' in the room that fronted the hall which was about

20 by 25 feet in dimensions, the regular dining room being entirely too small for the purpose. There were no courses whatsoever but it was a plain good breakfast without knick knacks."

Governor Morton hosted the meal for at least fourteen of Lincoln's companions, including his son Robert. They finished breakfast a little after 9:00 a.m. and went to the State House, where they met with members of the Legislature. A little before noon, Lincoln's party boarded the train on its way to Cincinnati. Mrs. Mary Todd Lincoln, Tad, and Willie had arrived on the train from Springfield, Illinois, to join Lincoln and son Robert. A large crowd was at the train station when the Lincolns boarded the train to leave. It is very likely that Lucinda met and greeted Mrs. Lincoln when she arrived.

The special train resumed its tour and Mrs. Lincoln and the boys stopped off in Harrisburg, Pennsylvania, while President Lincoln traveled on to Washington. The family reunited in Washington on February 23.

# Chapter 9

# DOMESTIC DUTIES

Keeping the Governor's House ready for guests was no small matter. Lucinda's sister, Eliza Holloway, was married to William Holloway, who had come to Indianapolis as Morton's private secretary. The Holloways lived at the Governor's House when they first came to Indianapolis. Eliza worked alongside Lucinda in taking care of guests who came to the Governor's Mansion. Their youngest sister, Sarah Burbank, also came to live at the Governor's House to help. She was single until her marriage to Captain Caleb Gill in 1865.

There was a lot of work to keeping house and preparing meals in the home of the 1860s. Fireplaces were still very much in use but only as needed for heating. Cooking and heating stoves had replaced the fireplace in the more affluent homes for the kitchen and the main rooms. Candles were still the main source of lighting; however, gas was being used in some public buildings, churches, and stores. Only the wealthy could afford gas lighting, and it was not available until near the end of the Civil War. Coal oil for lamps was beginning to be available in the late 1850s, but kerosene from oil was still in early stages of refining. The kerosene oil lamp was not widely used until after the Civil War.

All the water for cooking, washing dishes and clothes, and bathing had to be heated on the stove and carried where needed. The water would have to be pumped, and in most cases, carried into the house from an outdoor pump. Indianapolis had no water or sanitary systems in 1861. It was not the habit to take baths every day, but to wash up daily and bathe once a week. There were no bathrooms or sanitary arrangements except the family outhouse. The outhouse was a small building usually near the house in the backyard, just big enough for one or two persons. A pit was dug for the refuse and lime was often dropped into it to control the odor.

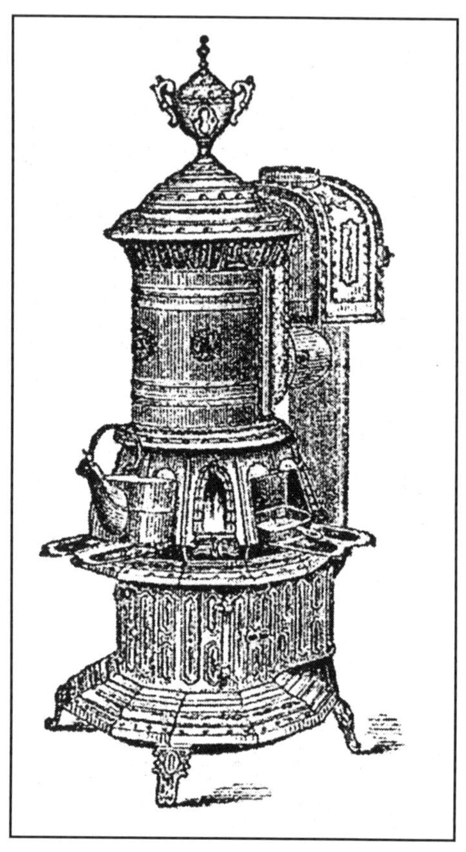

*A base burner parlor stove was used for heating.*

The kitchen stove was kept burning even in Indiana's hot summers to heat water, cook the food, and do the baking. The wood box had to be kept filled, which was usually the job of the boys. Coal was becoming available for the stoves. There was little refrigeration in hot weather unless there was a springhouse on the property. A springhouse is a separate small building covering a cool spring of running water. Water, milk, and other drinks could be kept cool by setting containers in the cold water. Food that did not require refrigeration could also be kept there for a short time. There was no springhouse on the Market Street property.

It is likely that ice could be purchased for an icebox in the kitchen. The damp basement was not cool enough for refrigeration. Meat (such as hams and bacon) was smoked and could be stored. Fresh meat was cooked fairly quickly.

Lucinda did not mention a vegetable garden, but most homes, even in the city, had gardens on their properties. The process for canning food in glass jars was in use by the time of the Civil War. Everything from meat to vegetables and fruit could be canned and stored. With grapes and cherries on the property, Lucinda and her sisters could can the fruit and make pies, juice, jams, and jellies. This was important for preparing foods quickly. The most popular fruits in Indiana were apples, peaches, pears, cherries, berries, and grapes and were readily available when in season. Fruit could also be dried and stored in a cool, dry place. A few foods were available in metal cans. Vegetables from the garden would include beans, potatoes, onions, carrots, and other vegetables. Root vegetables could be stored for several months. Herbs were grown and dried for seasoning.

Cleanliess was difficult for people in the 1860s. Lucinda had five in her family. Eliza's son, Edward, was born in 1861, while they were living with the Mortons, making three in their family. With their sister Sarah, it made nine people living at the house, two of them babies in diapers.

On Monday mornings, the washtubs were filled with hot water to wash and cool water for rinsing. There were no washing machines, just large tubs and scrubbing boards. Hand wringers could press out the excess water. If it was not raining, the clothes were hung on the outdoor clothesline. When the weather didn't cooperate, clothes were hung on drying racks placed by a stove, or hung on the porch, and sometimes in the attic, to dry. Almost every piece of clothing, tablecloths, napkins, sheets, etc. had to be ironed with flat irons that were heated on the stove. The dry, wrinkled clothes were sprinkled with water, rolled up, and each piece would be ironed while still damp. Fancy dresses were carefully brushed, spot cleaned, and pressed, and most had collars that could be removed to wash. Men's suits would be brushed to remove dirt and dust. Shirts had removable collars that could be washed so the shirt could be worn more than one day. Top hats would be carefully brushed and set on a shelf.

There were no personal deodorants, but there were perfumes and scented powders, soap and water. Smoke from stoves, fireplaces, and cooking odors can cling to clothing. It would have been a matter of pride that the clothing and linens of the Governor's family were clean and pressed and as free from odor as possible.

The Governor's House was on a busy street. Sweeping and dusting were always needed in the house of the 1860s. Brooms were used for sweeping, mops for dusting and washing the bare floors. A new invention of the handheld carpet sweeper made it easier to

*The carpet sweeper replaced the broom for many household cleaning jobs.*

clean the carpets. This was an everyday job because of the constant entertaining. Dirt from the gravel streets and sidewalks would be carried in every day. The streets were often muddy, and always dusty, from the passing carriages and wagons. Dust sifted through every crack. Keeping the house clean, doing the ironing, washing, repairing and making clothing, cooking, and housework was non-stop. Strong backs, strength, and energy were needed for both men and women. Even with the help of her sisters, Lucinda would have hired household helpers when it was too much for the family.

A stable on the property housed the carriage and horses with a carriage driver. The Governor's House was within walking distance from the State House, about one block. However, the horse and carriage were kept busy collecting guests at the railroad station and running errands for the household.

Lucinda continued her 1896 memories, "We lived very simply at all times and without the form that is in vogue nowadays. The fact of the matter is we could not have entertained as lavishly then as people do nowadays on the income from the Governor's office. We always had plenty to eat, however, and what we had was well cooked, but nothing was lavish."

While Lucinda did not think her meals were lavish, they were served with grace and proper social etiquette of the time. A typical dinner began with soup, a course with meat would follow, and end with dessert. The meat course might be fried chicken, with hot biscuits, cold ham, vegetable, and salads from greens that were in season.

"The table was always set for the next meal," Lucinda recalled. "A favorite dessert was a large cake in the center of the table with stands of jelly and float (a soft pudding). A pyramid cake or pretty iced cakes were favorites, and often we had pyramids of macaroons. Of course, these little table decorations varied with varying tastes."

There was no liquor served in the Governor's House. The Mortons were "temperate," meaning they did not serve alcohol and were in agreement with the strong temperance movement around the state. Coffee and tea were the main beverages served with meals. Cider and fruit drinks were served when in season.

"We could not be expected to put on many 'extras' when our guests were so numerous. Our carriage became known as the 'Governor's hack,' because it was at the station for some guest upon the arrival of almost every incoming train," recalled Lucinda.

Lucinda quickly gained the reputation of being a gracious hostess for the Governor's House and for her many guests. The Morton's two youngest children needed more attention than Lucinda was able to give them with all the demands of her position. John, at fifteen, would have been in school part of the year when he attended the White Water College in Centerville. Lists of students at the Centerville Collegiate Institute (the same school changed names in the 1860s) shows both Walter and Oliver attending there at a later date. John finished his early education in Centerville, staying with his Burbank relatives during the school sessions.

The two younger boys, Walter and Ollie (Oliver T.), were cared for by Sarah Backus McMahon. Sarah came from Ireland in 1854. In 1861, she married Thomas C. McMahon, who was in the army at Fort Benjamin Harrison. In consideration of Sarah and others in their employment who were of the Catholic faith, Morton arranged Sunday transportation and paid for a pew for them at Old St. John's Catholic Church. This is an example of Oliver and Lucinda's care for the well-being of their employees.

# Chapter 10

# GOVERNOR MORTON IN CHARGE

Governor Morton began his work at the Indiana State House immediately after his inauguration in 1861. He was the first Indiana-born citizen to serve as the Governor of Indiana. He also was the first Republican governor, ending the long period of nearly twenty years of Democrat governors. He was 37 years old and Lucinda was 35. Morton was among the youngest men to have served as Indiana's Governor at that time.

*Indiana Governor Oliver P. Morton.*

The State Capitol building, 200 West Washington Street, was just a short walk from the Governor's House on West Market Street. It was Indiana's first official building in Indianapolis to conduct the business of the state and was completed in 1835. The State

House design was Grecian Doric, except for the Italian Renaissance dome. The front faced south on Washington Street, and it stood on the south end of the present State House grounds.

The building was designed with an Executive suite, a Representative hall for 100 members, a Senate chamber for 50 members, rooms for the Supreme Court, Secretary of State, Auditor of State, the State Library, Law Library, and with six committee rooms and six clerks' rooms. It had been contracted for $48,000, but the building costs overran the original budget and cost $60,000. It was finished in time for the winter session of the 1835 legislature.

When David Wallace was serving as Governor, his young son Lew, a schoolmate of the Mortons, was a frequent visitor to the State Library. Originally, the library had been in the first Governor's Mansion on the Circle. It was mainly for use of lawyers and legislators. When the library was moved to the State House, it was separated from the Law Library. The State Library was opened to the public and was a favorite place for young Lew Wallace to borrow books. Lucinda Morton was also a lover of books. She, no doubt, would have borrowed from the library when they moved to Indianapolis.

After the Civil War, Lew Wallace became the author of *Ben-Hur: A Tale of Christ,* published in 1880. It is considered "the most influential Christian book of the nineteenth century," stated a writer for the National Endowment for the Arts in 2010.

The State Capitol building was considered a fine structure when it was built. It was 200 feet long and 100 feet wide. The dome and the rotunda were considered the most important parts of the building. Jacob P. Dunn, in his book on *Greater Indianapolis*, describes the importance of the public space of the rotunda (the large circular room in the State House under the dome) "… the rotunda is the one place where the citizen can feel at home, and glory in the fact that he is one of the masters of all these hirelings, and of the building."

Although the State House was impressive, it was not as sturdy

*A new State House in Indianapolis was completed in 1835. It was replaced by the current Capitol in 1888.*

as it looked. The foundation was of soft, blue buff limestone. The superstructure was part brick and part lath-covered wood. It was coated with stucco plaster, and neither the stone nor plaster could stand the extremes of Indiana weather. When Morton became Governor, the building was dilapidated, and according to Dunn, "It had been a public disgrace for several years." Attempts to repair and maintain the building were made, but it was considered unsafe. It eventually was demolished in 1877, to make room for the new Indiana State House, the one still in use today.

From the beginning of Morton's time as Governor, he had to deal with animosity, resentment, and hate over the situation created by states seceding from the Union. For several years, political parties and states had been sharply divided on the issue of extending slavery into new western states. Within a few months after Lincoln's election in November 1860, seven southern states had pulled away from the Union. In early February 1861, delegates from the seceding states met to create a new alliance called the Confederate States of America. They appointed Jefferson Davis as their President.

Efforts were made by the U.S. Legislature to halt the secession or to find a compromise, but all attempts had failed. Abraham Lincoln was inaugurated President of the United States on March 4, 1861.

He had to face the deteriorating national situation and make hard decisions. Governor Morton was convinced that the problems between the southern and the northern states would result in war. He had begun war preparations as soon as he became Governor. Although it was not unexpected, considering all the war talk, the firing on Fort Sumter was still a shock. Lucinda had always been interested in the current news. She would have been fully aware of her husband's anxiety about the political situation.

By the time Morton became Governor of Indiana in January 1861, hostilities between the Federal Government and the rebellious states had escalated. South Carolina and other seceding states seized Federal property within their borders, including all buildings and arsenals. On January 31, 1861, Governor Pickens of South Carolina demanded that President Buchanan surrender Fort Sumter because of its location in the Charleston Harbor. They had already captured the rest of the fortifications within their border. Fort Sumter was the only fort still occupied by Federal forces and it dominated the harbor.

Over the next months, South Carolina repeatedly called for evacuation of the fort, but it was ignored. The fort was running low on supplies, and a ship had been sent in early January to bring aid. As the ship approached Charleston Harbor, the South Carolina militia fired on it. The attack was too strong, and the supply ship turned back. All efforts to reach a compromise between the opposing forces failed, and war was imminent.

On Thursday, April 11, 1861, a final demand for surrender of Fort Sumter was made, but it was again refused. On Friday at 4:30 a.m., a bombardment of the fort began by the South Carolina militia against the small forces stationed there. It continued until Saturday, April 13, with the Union forces outmanned, outgunned, with dwindling supplies, and surrounded by enemy batteries. The fort surrendered about 2:30 p.m. and was evacuated. This first decisive battle against Union forces by the Confederates set off the anticipated War Between the States.

When word of the bombardment of Fort Sumter reached Indianapolis, there was an immediate flurry of excitement. On Saturday April 13, business was suspended and large crowds waited for the latest reports coming by telegraph. There was a mixture of excitement and anxiety about what this might mean for the state and the nation. Every city and town in Indiana had gatherings and patriotic meetings to express their loyalty to the President and the Union. According to some reporters, the state had "never before witnessed such hysteria."

On Saturday evening, mass meetings were held in Indianapolis. Two large halls were filled and there were still thousands on the streets. There was no division of political parties, but it appeared that all were in agreement for the need to defend the Union. Word came in the late evening that Fort Sumter had fallen. Governor Morton stayed at the telegraph office until the news came in about midnight.

The next day, Sunday, crowds in Indianapolis were again on the streets, and the churches were full. Ministers could not help but decry the war and urge their people to support the effort to save the Union.

President Lincoln's Proclamation was sent out that Sunday, April 15, calling for the militias of the states in the Union "to the aggregate number of seventy-five thousand, in order to suppress said combinations (Confederate States) and to cause the laws to be duly executed.... I appeal to all loyal citizens to favor, facilitate, and aid this effort to maintain the honor, the integrity, and the existence of our National Union and the perpetuity of popular government; and to redress wrongs, already so long endured."

## The War Begins

Indianapolis was on high alert with both excitement and dread for what was coming. "It would be impossible to describe the intensity of the feeling that the war news created in our city," according to the *Indiana State Sentinel* newspaper on April 17, 1861. Governor Morton had made speeches about the coming war even before becoming Governor, and newspapers had reported the talk of war for several weeks. It was well known that Morton had been preparing the state for the imminent possibility of hostilities across the nation.

*Civil War bulletin announcing news from Charleston. Courtesy of Indiana Historical Society.*

As soon as the proclamation was received, Morton quickly recruited men to help him lead the effort, appointing Lew Wallace as Adjutant General in charge of recruiting soldiers. Wallace was a member of the Democrat political party as Morton had been before he joined the Republican Party. Wallace, Morton, and Lucinda Morton had been schoolmates and friends for many years. Although the men came to disagree politically, there was still respect and friendship between them. Wallace offered his services to Morton as soon as the war started.

Lew Wallace had military experience, serving as an officer during the Mexican–American War, 1846–1848. After that, he continued to be interested in military life and had organized a military company in Crawfordsville in 1856, known as the Montgomery Guards. After studying the fighting tactics of a French unit from Algeria in North Africa called the Zouaves, Wallace outfitted and trained his company in the Zouave system. The Montgomery Guards' reputation for hard work and training grew, and by 1861, the company was considered the best military organization in Indiana.

Wallace agreed to help raise the six regiments requested by Lincoln on the condition that he could lead one of the regiments. He began immediately to recruit men for the army and prepared to raise his own regiment.

The *Marshall County Republican* newspaper on April 18, reported Wallace's call for a Zouave Regiment. "… I desire, if possible, to form a regiment of Zouaves, to consist of twelve companies of one hundred members. As soon as organized and accepted by the Governor, I propose, if time will allow it, to call … the officers in this city, and instruct them in the peculiar tactics in outpost duty, field fortifications, etc. The arms, uniforms, camp equipage, etc. will be purely Zouave in style.… Lew Wallace, Indianapolis, April 15, 1861."

Wallace had barely assumed his task when a letter was posted in the newspapers asking how women could help in the effort. The letter was signed by Lucinda Morton and friends. On April 17, the letter was published.

*General Lew Wallace*

*Dear Sir:*

*Please inform the ladies of this city how they can render some effectual service to the cause of the country. Will not the soldiers who rendezvous require clothing and blankets for their comfort?*

*The women of Indianapolis will not be wanting in every patriotic effort and sacrifice required of them in the hour of our country's peril. Will you let us hear from you at your earliest convenience?*

*Respectfully yours,*

*Lucinda M. Morton*

*Kate Ballard*

*E. H. Bates [Sister of Hervey Bates, Jr., owner of the Bates House Hotel]*

*Carolina Coburn [Wife of Congressman John Coburn]*

*Cordelia Wallace [Lew Wallace's sister-in-law]*

*On behalf of the ladies of Indianapolis*

The letter from the ladies of Indianapolis was answered swiftly as reported in the *Evansville Daily Journal*, April 20, 1861. Lucinda had immediately invited her friends to meet with her at the Governor's House to offer their service with the war effort. They sought guidance from the Adjutant General as to how they could best help.

*Adjutant General's Office*

*Ladies,*

*Your kind note of today asking 'how the ladies of your city can render some effectual service to the cause of the country,' came to me very opportunely. ... The soldier must have not merely your sympathy now, your tears at parting, and your prayers when he is in the field—he must have your practical aid, and have it right here. The nights are cold, the ground damp—see that he has blankets and bed clothing....*

Adjutant General Wallace went on to suggest other ways to help, such as supplies for the sick, although they might not be needed for months. He also encouraged the women not only to prepare supplies for soldiers in the field, but also to be involved in the needs of those in camp in Indianapolis. The response from Wallace was addressed to

Mrs. Governor Morton and the other ladies.

War efforts were moving forward rapidly, as volunteers from all over the state were coming to Indianapolis to join the army, including men and boys of all ages. There was the constant sound of martial music from the recruiting stations, frequent marches of companies through the streets, and the roar of cannons when recruits arrived on the trains. *The Daily Journal of Evansville* printed news from their Indianapolis correspondent. "We are here almost in a condition of a besieged city …"

According to a December 13, 1905 article in Richmond's *Indiana Morning Palladium* about the early days of the Civil War; on the day after Governor Morton's Proclamation, 50 men arrived in Indianapolis, the second day 2,400 more, and before the end of the week more than 12,000. They came by train, by horse, wagons, and on foot. Feeding and housing the men became a crisis, because Indianapolis and the state had no funds allotted and no place to put them.

As soon as recruits began to arrive in Indianapolis, Morton and Wallace looked for places for the men to stay. The only place with even basic requirements was the new State Fair Grounds. It was established in 1852, but only one State Fair had been held there. By 1861, several buildings had been built on the grounds, mostly for horses and livestock. On April 17, as volunteers were enlisting, the grounds were put into operation as a camp for housing and training them. No troops had yet been sent out by April 19, but about 1,500 men had enlisted, with others arriving constantly. Tents were quickly erected on the site. The camp was called Camp Morton.

Since calls were made for the help of the ladies, a correspondent reported that the "ladies, under Mrs. Morton's generalship, are plying the needle for them," to provide clothing and blankets for the soldiers.

Lucinda described the activities of the women as they began their work to help the soldiers. They met at the Governor's House on West Market Street.

"It soon became evident that we women should do something. We began with a sewing society, organized at my home and from this there were made district societies about the city. I was made President of the parent society. Mrs. Coburn, wife of General Coburn, and Mrs. Anna Beggs were among the active members."

"We started by making two large flags, but soon found it was more important to make clothing for the soldiers and to knit socks for those who were in the hospital."

Two regimental flags, made by the ladies of Indianapolis and Terre Haute, were presented to Lew Wallace's 11th Regiment, Indiana Volunteer Infantry, by Mrs. Cady. She had embroidered a beautiful golden eagle on the dark blue regimental colors. The patriotic event was held on May 8, 1861, as the regiment was preparing to leave for a 3-month enlistment, the first to go to war from Indiana. Lucinda and her sewing society were prominent guests.

The presentation of the flags was held on the grounds of the Indiana State House, with the 11th Indiana Regiment in their splendid Zouave

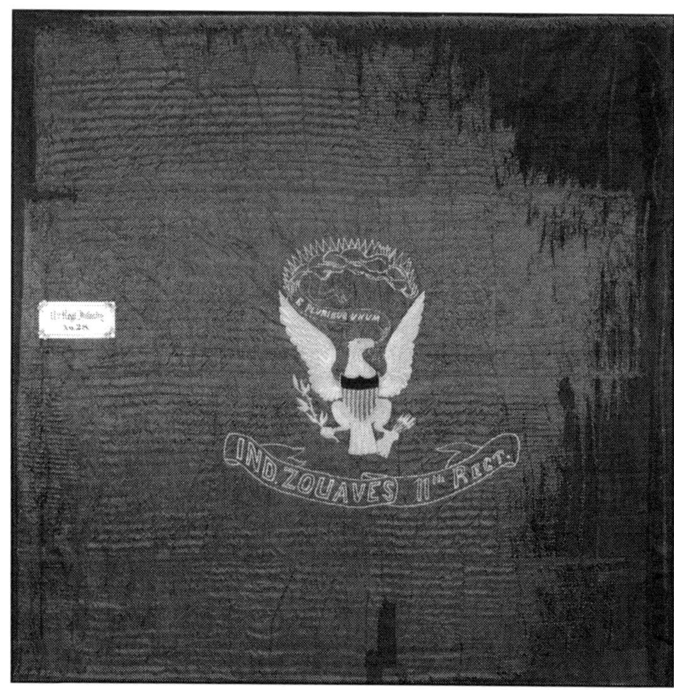


*One of 11th Indiana Infantry Regiment's regimental (blue standard) flags. The 11th Indiana Volunteer Infantry Regiment was also known as "Wallace's Zouaves." Image Courtesy of The Indiana War Memorials Commission.*

*General Lew Wallace receiving the regimental flags on the steps of the first State House. Courtesy of General Lew Wallace Study and Museum.*

uniforms. The grounds were crowded with hundreds of people, who enjoyed patriotic music and singing.

*Harper's Weekly*, June 22, 1861, reported that Colonel Wallace accepted the flags from Mrs. Cady and thanked the ladies. He turned and dramatically presented the colors to his troops. He said to them, "Will you ever desert the banners that have been presented to us today?" The deafening response was "Never! Never!"

Colonel Wallace ordered his men to kneel and swear, with their right arms lifted high, that they would stand by their country and its flag and to "Remember Buena Vista." This last alluded to the poor treatment of Indiana soldiers by Jefferson Davis, President of the Confederacy, in the War with Mexico. "Remember Buena Vista" became the motto of the regiment.

Colonel Wallace then presented Almina, the little daughter of Captain Smith, an officer of the regiment. Wallace asked the Zouaves if they would adopt the girl as the "daughter" of their regiment. A thunderous shout of "We will!" came from the young men, eager to get started on their new adventure.

Funds were collected and materials were purchased for ladies' patriotic groups to make into blankets and clothing. Women's societies and ladies' church groups in Indianapolis and other Indiana communities quickly joined the effort. Sewing machines, sewing needles, knitting needles, looms, and crochet hooks were in motion whenever ladies had time. Finished supplies began coming to the recruiting camps in short order.

An announcement in the *Indiana State Sentinel* on August 24, 1861, stated that the Ladies' Patriotic Association of Indianapolis had received the sum of $194.90 in donations. It had paid for materials for two flags and flannel for shirts, the total cost being $204.66. Some of the money pledged had not been received to cover the cost. However, liberal donation of flannel and muslin came from merchants and citizens for the ladies to make into bedding and clothing.

Preparations to supply needs of the soldiers went into high gear all over the state. *The Crawfordsville Weekly Journal* reported news of their local patriotic ladies on April 25, 1861.

"… 2 or 3 hundred ladies of Crawfordsville gathered at the McClelland's and Temperance Halls on Saturday (April 20) for the purpose of manufacturing tents, etc. for Captain Manson's company of volunteers which left on Monday morning. 20 or 30 sewing machines, both Saturday and Sunday, worked. Some 17 tents were pitched on the Public Square during the Sabbath."

The needs of the recruits at Camp Morton were not just for clothing. Three days after the camp opened, the Commissary General of the Indiana Militia urgently requested help with food for the camp and those soon to be on the march. He asked for salt pork or beef, sides of bacon, hams, and pork shoulders in barrels, casks, or boxes. Also needed were white beans, dried apples and peaches in barrels or sacks, crackers in barrels, hard soap, tallow, or candles in boxes.

"The war spirit which now rages like a prairie fire, is not likely to be crushed," according to an advertisement for Hammer's Sumptuous Lunches. "Everyone was trying to get into the act and push the war effort."

After the fall of Fort Sumter, there seemed to be little disagreement but that the state should support Lincoln and the Union. However, trade with rebel southern states was soon disrupted on the Kentucky and Indiana border and on the Ohio River. There was a strong pushback from farmers and businesses in southern Indiana. They saw their financial situation threatened and their southern relatives in danger. Concerns over new rules and restrictions began to bring about more disapproval. It was not long before Morton's enemies and political rivals were at work to challenge his leadership.

No matter what was going on with the politics, care of the recruits was an ongoing concern for Morton, his staff, and Lucinda. The first recruits who gathered at Indianapolis came only with what they could carry from home, mostly warm weather clothing. Enlistments for the solders were for three months. It was expected that the war would not last very long. It soon became clear that the combat would last much longer than the middle of the summer of 1861, and enlistments were increased to three years.

While only grown men were expected to enlist, the patriotic fever excited boys who tried to join. Young boys were only allowed to be musicians and the minimum age for a boy to sign up was twelve years old. For boys under the age of eighteen, it was necessary to have signed permission from a parent or guardian. It was not unusual to learn of parents forcefully removing their young son from recruitment for having falsely produced a permit. Even Lucinda may have been concerned that their son John, at fifteen, might be drawn by the excitement and try to enlist. Although John was nearly twenty by the end of the war, he did not serve in the military.

Lucinda and Oliver's middle son, Walter, did try to join the army. He was six years old when the war started. Patriotic music, marching soldiers, troop trains arriving and leaving, kept Indianapolis in a constant military atmosphere. Boys were enticed by the excitement. In 1893, the grown-up Walter was invited to a meeting of the Loyal Legion of St. Paul, Minnesota, an organization of Civil War Veterans. The gathering was attended by a large number of distinguished guests and veterans. After the supper, Lieutenant John Thornburgh of the Fourth Indiana Cavalry read a paper on "Oliver Perry Morton, the Great War Governor." He finished to loud applause and was given a vote of thanks for his valuable paper.

After Captain Cross gave another eloquent tribute to Governor Morton, his son, Walter Morton, was introduced and invited to speak. He spoke about his father and related stories from his youth. He said the bright spot in his boyhood days was that relating to his brief career in the army. He had run away as a small boy and was brought back from camp by his parents. Walter concluded his talk by thanking them for the touching and eloquent tributes paid to his father.

# Chapter 11

# THE LADIES' PATRIOTIC ASSOCIATION

At first, women at home did not know what or how much would be needed for the soldiers. Many women still made most of the family's clothing and bedclothes and were skilled at making all kinds of other things. They knew how to prepare food that would last without refrigeration. So women of the state started doing whatever they thought might be useful, such as the ladies of Crawfordsville making tents and clothing for their hometown regiment. There were many items produced and sent that were not useful for soldiers, but the ladies made whatever they thought might help and sent it to Indianapolis.

Uniforms were in short supply for several months and help was needed to outfit the troops. Similar color clothing was essential in battle to be able to recognize their comrades from the enemy. Several regiments, such as Lew Wallace's Zouaves, had their own distinctive uniforms. The Zouave uniform was basically a short jacket, vest, baggy pants, sash, and boots. Seventy Zouave regiments served in the Union army, and each had its own version of the uniform.

There were different types of hats, including the havelock, a hat with cloth or material attached to the back. It was designed for British and French troops while serving in hot climates and for protection from the sun on the back of the neck. Much of the war was being fought in the hot summer of 1861, and it seemed the havelock would be a good thing for the Union troops.

The ladies of Indianapolis organized their sewing society, known as the Indianapolis Ladies' Patriotic Association, with branches in each ward. Mrs. Morton was the President and some of the ladies met at her home. They made blankets, shirts, and other garments, and havelocks. A havelock was easy to construct by adding material to the back of the kepi hat that was the standard issue for the regular army. In

HARPER'S WEEKLY.
A JOURNAL OF CIVILIZATION.
Vol. V.—No. 235.] NEW YORK, SATURDAY, JUNE 29, 1861.

*The cover illustration on the June 29, 1861 issue of "Harper's Weekly" depicts women sewing havelocks for the Union Army.*

their enthusiasm to help, sewing groups made large numbers of them. However, the soldiers said it was hot and didn't let air circulate around their necks. By 1862, the havelock had fallen out of favor.

In the fall of 1861, Indiana soldiers were engaged in fighting in various parts of the country. All gear for the troops was in short supply. The government was not able to purchase needed goods because they were not available. Also, the federal government would not pay for everything that was needed. Recognizing that winter was coming with no end to the war, Morton took action and issued a call in the newspapers on October 10, 1861.

*To the Patriotic Women of Indiana:*

> *When the President issued his first call to the loyal States for help, the government was unprovided with most, if not all, of the articles necessary to the comfort and health of soldiers in the camp and in the field. The women of Indiana were appealed to, and they supplied the deficiency in our State with a generous alacrity, which entitles them to the gratitude of the nation. The approach of winter makes it necessary to appeal to them again. Our volunteers, already suffering from exposure, against which they are inadequately protected, will soon be compelled to endure the most severity of winter and multiplied dangers of disease ...*

Morton continued listing things that the soldiers would need, such as two or three pairs of good strong socks, wool gloves and mittens, woolen shirts, and underwear. Blankets could not be purchased and the supply was already exhausted. His appeal was to the numerous female benevolent societies as well as women who had no opportunities to join these organizations.

The finished articles were to be sent to the Quartermaster General of the State, with a card stating the name and address of the donor and where they would like their things to be sent, if they had a request. This information would be recorded. This was the first organized effort of any state to make special provision for its own soldiers. The response by Indiana women brought a large outpouring of the suggested articles as well as other "comforts" for the troops.

That same fall, Morton had seen with his own eyes the need for warm winter clothing for the soldiers in the mountains of Virginia. He arranged to purchase overcoats for the Indiana soldiers. It took much pressure, cajoling, and tolerating red tape by Morton before they were finally purchased and distributed to the Indiana troops.

In November 1861, the Ladies' Patriotic Association was reorganized and Lucinda was again named its President. Before, it had only been loosely organized ladies' groups in Indianapolis. It had become clear that the war would last much longer than first expected. A more organized system of preparing supplies was needed and it was important to know what was being made for the troops and what would be needed.

The care and feeding of the troops was just one of the complex issues confronting Governor Morton. At the time Morton became Governor, the state had very little money because of debt, poor management, and a number of frauds perpetrated against the state. This lack of state funds caused Morton no end of grief as the legislature was mixed in its willingness to appropriate funds, borrow money, and collect back taxes. Through his own network of influential bankers, wealthy friends, and businessmen, Morton was able to borrow large sums of money on his own personal credit to help the state out of its financial hole.

The Federal Union Army was poorly prepared for war and Indiana could not find a source for guns and ammunition. Two weeks after the fall of Fort Sumter, Morton appointed Herman Strum to the task of running a state arsenal in Indianapolis. It produced ammunition for field pieces and small arms. Morton worked closely with his staff to see that the soldiers were supplied with what they needed, as each regiment was being formed, trained, and sent out. Besides the efforts for the soldiers, Governor Morton worked on state legislative affairs.

He made trips to visit the battlefields and to Washington to consult with Lincoln. He worked long hours and into the night to keep things moving.

Lucinda took on as much responsibility as she could to help. She handled their personal finances and the details of the Governor's House. Morton took little thought for his own well-being and health. He often ate at odd times and whatever was offered. His clothing and dress were of no concern to him, but Lucinda made sure he was dressed properly and was well groomed. As more responsibilities piled on her husband, she could not help but worry. Threats of violence against him began to appear. Many nights, Lucinda would turn out the house lights, except for a candle in the window, and wait up until he was safely at home.

The winter of 1861–1862 was coming on and the call went out for more food and clothing for the soldiers. Lucinda had many friends who gladly assisted her, serving on committees and wherever they were needed. The war effort dominated everything, but social affairs continued to be important. Receptions, dinners, and other entertainments were popular. It was through these events and her leadership of the Ladies' Patriotic Association that Lucinda became the social leader of Indianapolis. The customs observed by the Governor's wife were soon the "common law" of the city's social circles. Lucinda was always described as a gentle and considerate hostess. The many social events, as well as hosting government officials, kept the Governor's House constantly busy and in the spotlight of the news.

## Indianapolis

Indianapolis began to change rapidly. Hundreds of men and boys, sometimes with their families, came to enlist and to be trained. This, and the growth of new business, increased the city's population. In 1860, Indianapolis had 18,611 residents, and by the end of 1864, it had grown to 45,000. This increased the need for new construction of commercial buildings and homes. Property values grew so rapidly that it astonished the buyers and housing was difficult to find. Higher prices raised the income of producers of wheat, corn, hogs, and manufactured goods. By the end of 1862, inflation had increased prices on everything, some as much as 75%. While some people's wealth increased, many others struggled with the rise in the cost of living, especially those whose breadwinners had gone to war.

Important changes for Indianapolis and the state included the growth of the railroads and their importance for shipping products, troops, and supplies for the war effort. New factories were built, and there was work for anyone who wanted it because so many young men were serving in the war. Along with the growing wealth in Indianapolis came crime, fraudulent schemes to swindle soldiers and newcomers, drunkenness, and unsafe streets.

With the increase in crime, the policemen of Indianapolis were uniformed in 1862, so that their presence in an area would be recognized as a warning to lawbreakers. Until this time, the only sign of their office was a star badge. The new uniforms were dark blue coats and pants with a stripe down the side, similar to the soldier's uniform.

Lucinda was very busy with her family, her hostess duties, and the Ladies' Patriotic Association. She kept abreast of the war news and the society news through the local newspapers. Lists of the soldiers who were wounded or died in battle and those who were ill, were printed and prominently displayed in the windows of newspaper offices. These lists were updated often, and there was a constant flow of people standing at the windows looking for news about their family members. Lucinda would often share the grief of widows, children, and parents of those who had loved ones on the lists. No one was exempt from the human cost of the war.

The two leading newspapers in Indianapolis were the *Indiana State Sentinel* and the *Indiana Daily Journal*. The *Sentinel* became the voice of the Indiana Democrats and stated that it was the "friend of sound National principles to aid them in that object. The *Sentinel* will take for its political guide the National and State Democratic Platform and earnestly advocate the principles and policies they maintain."

The *Journal* supported the Republican policies of President Lincoln and Governor Morton. Strong editorials in both papers championed their points of view. Speeches of politicians were often printed in full length. Whenever something was important to announce to the public, it was printed in both papers, such as Morton's call for the ladies' help or information for the recruits. War news filled the papers, both sides expressing their pleasure or disappointment at how the war was going.

There was no sparing of feelings for anyone who was in the critical eye of the newspapers. Governor Morton was often the topic of either support from the *Journal* or bitter accusations from the *Sentinel*. Both Morton and Lucinda were avid readers of newspapers, magazines, and books. She could not have helped but see the articles criticizing anything and everything about the war effort. But she knew Morton worked very hard. He considered Lucinda an intelligent and capable companion. From their earliest days of marriage, she had been his sounding board for ideas and speeches. She knew that in his heart he had the best interest of the soldiers and the state.

As soon as Indiana regiments were sent out, Morton was involved in being sure the troops were well provided for. He continued to visit battlefields, hospitals, and supply depots to see for himself. Later, a system of agents traveled with supplies to see to their distribution and to the care of soldiers from Indiana. The war grew more intense and was not an easy win for the Union army. Morton's enemies of Southern sympathizers, Peace Democrats, and radical abolitionists of his own party increased their attacks against him. He received death threats. His political adversaries worked against him in the State Legislature, Democratic newspapers ridiculed him, and he was often at odds with Washington as to how the war was being run. In spite of all this, Morton kept doing what he thought best.

# Chapter 12

# INDIANA'S SANITARY COMMISSION

The year 1862 brought new challenges as the war dragged on with no sign of ending. Governor Morton and Lucinda's concern for the soldiers never wavered. There had been some effort by the Federal Government to feed and take care of the soldiers on the fighting field, but there was never enough. In order to meet these needs, the United States Sanitary Commission had been set up in June 1861, to collect supplies for the Union army. However, the Commission took no special interest in individual state regiments and Morton was greatly concerned for the Indiana

*Women working at a Post Office to aid the Sanitary Commission.*

soldiers. In February 1862, Morton established the Indiana Sanitary Commission and the Indiana Military Agency for the benefit of Indiana soldiers. The Sanitary Commission collected the supplies and the Military Agency distributed them to Indiana's troops serving on the battlefield.

Morton did not hold back his opinions with Washington officials about the war. He found himself at odds with those in charge, especially when the needs of the soldiers were involved. However, when things went as he thought they should, there was no stronger advocate for the war effort than Governor Morton.

## Camp Morton

In that same month of February, several thousand Confederate soldiers were taken captive at the fall of Fort Donelson on the Tennessee and Kentucky border, a major victory for the Union army. Morton was asked to take some of the prisoners and house them in Indianapolis. Camp Morton was immediately turned into a prison

*Prisoners in Camp Morton in Indianapolis.*

camp. Governor Morton agreed to take 2,000 prisoners, but in a few days the number had grown to over 4,000. Other places than Indianapolis had to be found to take the overflow.

The arrival of the Confederate prisoners was seen as a hopeful sign that the Union was winning the war. It also brought the reality of the war to Indiana. The winter weather was extremely cold, and the prisoners were poorly clothed. Many were ill with wounds, camp diseases, and deprivations brought on by the war. As soon as the desperate condition of the prisoners was known, the women of the city were called on for their help. Even the women of the Democratic Party, who had before refused to help, joined the effort to provide for the prisoners. As before, the Ladies' Patriotic Association was quick to prepare supplies, clothing, bedding, and food for Camp Morton and the sick. Business places gave food and other goods, and there was a generous attitude toward the prisoners at that time. However, the need of the prisoners was much greater than the ability to provide, so there was much suffering and death among them.

Efforts on behalf of the prisoners were not without controversy. There were many Southern sympathizers in Indiana and they were looked on with suspicion. Some of the ladies with Union sympathies were concerned about helping the prisoners, as they also might come under suspicion of being for the Confederacy.

The Christ Church Cathedral on Monument Circle is one of the oldest religious organizations in Indianapolis. It was organized in 1837 as the Episcopal Diocese of Indianapolis, Christ Church parish. A second church was built in 1857–1859 on the same location as the first church. Horace Stringfellow, Jr., served as the rector of the church from 1860–1863. He was a Southerner and during the Civil War, feelings on political differences ran high. A number of prominent Democrats were in his congregation and their political enemies wrote and said many critical things about them.

When the call came to help the Confederate prisoners in Camp Morton, Mr. and Mrs. Stringfellow furnished some food to the rebel prisoners. The Republican newspaper, *The Indiana Journal*, and others immediately criticized their actions in the most bitter and hateful way. It caused so much turmoil and contention that Stringfellow felt his usefulness as rector was at an end, and he handed in his resignation in 1863. The church congregation begged him to stay and his vestry publicly expressed confidence in him. They condemned the injustice of the criticism, but he insisted upon leaving. The consequences of even appearing to be a Southern sympathizer were harsh.

On February 19, 1862, Lucinda made an urgent request in the newspaper for hospital supplies, calling each of the Ward Societies and each Soldier's Aid Society "to please attend immediately to this call, and will not the ladies all promptly and heartily respond?" Help was needed for the "comfort of our wounded brave." This call came just before the first prisoners of war arrived on February 22. No doubt, this newspaper call helped to meet the needs of both the Union sick and wounded and the Confederate prisoners.

## A Train Wreck

The Indiana Sanitary Commission sent out its first supply train on Saturday night, May 11, 1862, from Indianapolis for Terre Haute. The train's route was to head south through southern Indiana to Corinth, Mississippi where a battle was expected. Morton and four or five others were aboard the train. The train was filled with a large amount of food and supplies for the sick and suffering soldiers at Pittsburg Landing, Corinth, and vicinity. The train raced along the tracks at the speed of 24 miles per hour. When it reached Sullivan, Indiana, a terrible crash wrecked the train.

One of Morton's companions on the train was Miles Fletcher, 31, the State Superintendent of Education. He had been elected at the same time as Morton. Morton invited Miles' father, Calvin Fletcher, but he was unable to take the trip, so he asked his son to take his place. Calvin Fletcher, a banker, was the largest taxpayer in Marion County, one of Indiana's richest men, and a generous supporter of the war effort.

The train accident was caused by Milton Belser and his friend, James Dooley. They had attended a party in the town of Sullivan and perhaps had imbibed of alcohol. Late on that Saturday evening, they had conspired to move a freight car from its place on a sidetrack. Belser, on leave from the 31st regiment of Indiana volunteers, said he wanted to take a ride on the old boxcar if he could move it. He managed to push the car onto the crossties of the main track. James Dooley stated to the coroner's jury that he was only a bystander and that he suggested they try to get it off the track. Belser said there were no trains due, that the boxcar should cause no problem, and that someone would move it back on Sunday.

The supply train had been moving steadily on the tracks in the middle of the night, not expecting a problem. Suddenly, about one o'clock in the morning, the engine struck the boxcar with a fearful crash, breaking and almost demolishing it and the locomotive. The few men traveling with Morton had been asleep. Morton and Fletcher were sleeping on long passenger benches next to the car windows. They jumped up at the loud sound. Fletcher opened a window and put his head out. His head was immediately struck by the remains of the boxcar and he was killed instantly.

*A painting of Miles Fletcher by Indiana artist T. C. Steele.*

Torn between grief of the tragic death of his young friend Miles Fletcher and the urgent need for the supplies, Morton arranged for the body to be taken back to Indianapolis on a special train. He personally wrote a letter to Miles' father, explaining the accident and sending his condolences. Another train was brought to take the supplies on to the battlefield and Morton continued with it. The supply train would bring back the sick and wounded to be taken to hospitals in Indiana.

The accident scene in Sullivan drew big crowds to see the wreck. It was widely speculated that this was no accident, but a planned attempt to kill Morton. He also felt that the train wreck might have been the work of his enemies, especially when it happened at an Indiana town with many Southern sympathizers.

The death of Miles Fletcher was investigated locally in Sullivan and declared an accident and not an attempt to wreck the train. It was widely believed that the Coroner's jury was made up of Southern sympathizers who had no intention of declaring the incident anything but an accident. Milton Belser went back to his regiment after having been declared guilty, but with no punishment. But for many of Morton's supporters, this was likely an attempt to kill him and wreck the supply train.

It would have been Lucinda's sad duty to attend the funeral and send their condolences. The Fletcher families were longtime friends of the Mortons. Miles Fletcher had given as much of his time as he could to help with the war effort. He had a young family and was respected in his role as State Superintendent of Education. Samuel Hoshour, Morton's old friend and mentor, was appointed to finish Miles' term until the next election.

This latest accident or suspected attack involving Morton and the death of their young friend must have been very upsetting for Lucinda. She would have felt the deep grief of her close friends. Although she supported Morton's travels to aid the soldiers and his trips to Washington, they caused her no end of anxiety for his safety. She was aware of his many death threats. But Morton dismissed the train accident as not being an attempted assassination and tried to shield Lucinda from hearing about other threats. But as soon as the newspaper reporters had any information about threats and attempts on his life, it was printed and Lucinda would learn of it.

# Chapter 13

# MID-TERM ELECTION OF 1862

The next big challenge was the mid-term election of 1862. Morton had shown his organizational skills and his ability to get things done in spite of opposition. This infuriated his Democrat enemies and the radical Republicans in the State. George Julian, of Centerville, an Indiana representative in Congress, was a strong and outspoken abolitionist. His brother Isaac Julian's newspaper, *The True Republican,* in Centerville, was critical of Morton and his policies because Morton did not make the abolition of slavery his main concern. Although they were in the same political party, Morton and Julian rarely agreed on anything.

The war was not going well for the Union in the summer of 1862. Many soldiers were ill, wounded, killed, or ended up in prison camps. Large numbers of soldiers deserted. To those at home who lost loved ones or their men were wounded, the losses were heartbreaking. Southern sympathizers used these doubts and insecurities to work against President Lincoln and Morton. Governor Morton and the Indiana Republicans were blamed for the military draft, which was very unpopular. Although Morton was not up for reelection, his support for state candidates was not strong enough to keep the Republicans in control of the Indiana Legislature.

As soon as the Democrats took control of the Legislature in 1863, they fought Morton on every front. He could not get state funding for critical areas of the war effort. It was becoming a financial crisis for how Indiana was to continue the support for their soldiers. With no consensus or votes in the Legislature on important bills, Morton, out of frustration, took matters into his own hands and set up agencies and people to operate without the approval of the Legislature.

Every detail of supplies purchased and money borrowed for the war was carefully recorded. Morton called on business, banks, and community support from around the state. He used his own credit to borrow money from wealthy friends to help the state pay its bills and interest on loans. He looked for any way possible to obtain the money for the war effort.

Imagine how distressed Lucinda must have been as she recognized the risks her husband was taking. He was risking everything, politically and financially, and their own resources, by operating the state's financial affairs without the agreement of the Legislature. There was no way she could be kept in the dark about the problems facing Morton and the state.

The Democrat newspapers, the *Indiana State Sentinel* and others across the state, were full of accusations and complaints. Morton was accused of being a tyrant and a dictator. Only those around him realized what a terrible strain it was for him to try to hold things together.

The war continued on without much progress, and feelings were strong against the Republicans and Morton at the time of the mid-term election. The threats were so constant that Morton arranged military guards for the State House. The *Sentinel* sneered at the Governor's use of soldier guards and reported, "to reach his office one had to pass the soldier armed with the bayonet. The men enlisted to defend the integrity of the Union were employed as a bodyguard about his sacred person." It is not clear if Morton employed personal bodyguards, but he and his family were threatened almost the whole time he was Governor.

The *Plymouth Weekly Democrat* picked up the complaint about guards, saying, "Our readers will be astonished to learn that O. P. Morton, following the example of his highness, Old Abe, has a body guard in attendance upon himself at all hours during the day, and a guard around his house at night" and accused Morton of "an unmanly, despicable cowardice."

## Emancipation

On January 1, 1863, President Lincoln's proclamation and his executive order, The Emancipation Proclamation, went into effect. It

*A poster showing the Emancipation Proclamation.*

had been issued on September 22, 1862. The proclamation stated: "all persons held as slaves within the rebellious states are, and henceforth shall be free." Before that in 1861, Congress had passed a bill declaring that all slaves employed against the Union were free. The slaves that had come to the North were already considered free.

Governor Morton was among the first state governors to support Lincoln's proclamation, although he had not been an active advocate for the abolition of slavery and had not become embroiled in this issue. Morton was severely criticized by George Julian and his radical group of Republicans in Washington and Indiana, for not actively supporting the abolition cause. Julian, a native of Centerville, served in the U.S. House of Representatives from 1861–1870. Morton did not agree with or support Julian, but worked against his reelection in 1870, and Julian lost the election. Governor Morton, and later, Senator Morton, was a force to be reckoned with by his political enemies.

The winter of 1862–1863 was extremely cold, causing the soldiers, their families at home, and the prisoners at Camp Morton more suffering. Again the people of Indianapolis and the state, and particularly the Ladies' Patriotic Association, were called upon for help. Lucinda immediately called for ladies to help provide food, clothing, and blankets for the soldiers and the prisoners. Although there was an outpouring of help, it was impossible to meet all the needs and the cruel cold caused great suffering.

Most of the people of Indianapolis were respectful of the prisoners. The Confederate sympathizers kept up their harassment and complaints about the treatment of the prisoners. Some people continued to be afraid to give help openly to Camp Morton because they might be accused of sympathizing with the South. They feared retaliation against themselves, their businesses, and families. But Lucinda Morton did not let up urging women to continue helping with the many poorly clothed, sick, wounded, and hungry men. Whenever she felt that more help was needed, she put articles in both the *Journal* and *Sentinel* newspapers, urging the ladies to go back to work. Lucinda's articles were quickly picked up and printed in other newspapers around the state. Her encouragement always brought a wave of more help.

# Chapter 14

# THE SOLDIERS' HOME

With Camp Morton filled with prisoners, there was no place for soldiers to stay when returning home or coming through the city. Soldiers' pay was small and most of it went to help their families at home. They had little money to provide for themselves when they arrived on the trains. The need was great and it was decided to build a Soldiers' Home close to the railroad station so that the returning men could have shelter and food. The Soldiers' Home was opened in August 1863, and was supported by the Sanitary Commission.

In early 1863, the state of Morton's personal finances was of great concern to him. The time was nearing when he would either have to run for election or not.

On June 29, he met with banker Calvin Fletcher to discuss what he should do. He told Fletcher of his money problems—that the coming election would cost a lot and he could not bear the expense. If the money could not be raised for him, he would have to resign. Just that day, Lucinda had to give up her carriage and horse. The Governor's House was still being visited by soldiers, their wives, and children every day, and they could not turn them away without giving them help.

Fletcher suggested that Morton contact some of his friends to help, but Morton was only willing to suggest Judge Elijah Martindale, who was a close adviser to him. Fletcher followed up by contacting men to help raise the money for Morton. He was willing to give money himself because he wanted to see Morton continue as Governor. The election for governor was over a year later, but this gave time for sufficient funds to be collected.

Even though the Soldiers' Home in Indianapolis had opened, not everyone knew about it. With so many people still coming for help to the Governor's House, Morton was prompted by Lucinda to established a "Ladies' Home" to care for the visiting families of soldiers. It opened in December 1863, and was under the care of the Sanitary Commission.

Before and during the winter of 1863, many women, sometimes with children, came to Indianapolis to see their loved ones. With information about their men so hard to come by, family members assumed they would be able to visit hospitals or help out somehow. The women came with little or no money and no means to provide for themselves. They needed constant help and applied to the State officers or the Sanitary Commission, but there was little aid available. The funds were irregular and inadequate for the emergency.

Lucinda knew this problem firsthand when she told of how the Governor's House was seen at the beginning of the war. "The people of the State had somewhat different ideas of what the Governor's House should be from those that are held now. In those days, soldiers' wives and their children came to the Governor's House to stay all night, sometimes to remain for a day or two. We could not send them to a hotel as they had no money. They seemed to think it was our duty to entertain them. We had quite enough to do in that time with entertaining guests who came from a distance...."

Soon Lucinda had to refuse to take care of soldiers' families when they came to her house. She was sympathetic to their desire to learn about loved ones in the army, but it was impossible to make room for them or financially provide for them. The opening of the Ladies'

Home solved that problem for visiting soldiers' families.

There was constant communication by letters and telegrams between Morton and Washington. Whenever he felt it urgent, Morton traveled to Washington to meet with the President and military leaders. He did not hold back his suggestions and continued to request more help with supplies for the soldiers. When he could not get what was needed, he took it on himself to see that it was done. His critics and enemies never let up in their war of words against Morton. Only his strong will and commitment to the war effort kept Morton from paying attention to his critics.

Lucinda knew and understood her husband's struggles. She read the attacks in the press and knew about the difficulties with the State Legislature. But she continued to do what she could and frequently reported the progress of the various ladies' groups in the newspapers.

The business of the war was constantly in the forefront of everyone's minds. The Mortons occasionally took a brief rest from the tensions of the war by attending performances at the Metropolitan Hall, which was near the Governor's House. Almost as if there were no war worries, the Indianapolis theaters were popular and filled for all performances by soldiers and local residents. Mrs. Morton spoke of having attended a play starring John Wilkes Booth. He later murdered their friend, President Lincoln.

Social life at the Governor's House rarely let up. The dining table was set, ready for guests at all times. Many government officials came to Indianapolis to confer with Morton. They were entertained with dinners and receptions. Often, they stayed as overnight guests or for a day or two. Secretary of the Treasury Salmon Chase, Secretary of War Simon Cameron, and other members of President Lincoln's Cabinet stayed with them. Generals and Senators came to meet with Governor Morton and were entertained. According to Lucinda, … "no one of special prominence came to Indianapolis without becoming our guest before he took his departure."

Lucinda was a popular hostess and the social leader of Indianapolis. In her interview of 1896 for *The Indiana Woman,* she names several prominent members of Indianapolis society, including General and Mrs. Benjamin Harrison. The people Lucinda mentioned were not only friends and leaders of society, but were active on committees and in efforts to help with the civilian war work.

At the beginning of 1863, Morton's salary had been increased to $3,000. This was double the amount of the Governor's salary when he came into office. The Governor's salary increase had been passed by the Legislature before the Democrats took over. It still did not meet the rising costs, the needs of his family, or of the expense of entertaining in the Governor's House. Lucinda had to use much of their own resources to pay the bills. The rising prices of everything made the raise in salary barely adequate, even with Lucinda's careful management.

Morton and Lucinda were concerned about the poor condition of the house they were living in. Even with all the improvements, it was still cold, damp, and drafty. They wondered whether they should continue to live there, considering all the illnesses the family and staff had suffered. On May 6, 1863, Morton sold his Centerville house to his first Secretary of State, William A. Peele, for $4,500. Peele wanted the house for his family as he planned to return to Centerville to practice law after his term of service was over. The money from the sale of the Centerville house and the increase in salary allowed them to look for a different place to live in Indianapolis.

It was the custom of Governor Morton to work long after hours at his office in the State House. Late one evening in the summer of 1863, as he started the short walk to his house, a shot rang out, shattering the silence of the quiet night. It missed its mark but came very close to Morton's head. He took refuge in the Bates House Hotel that was a little closer than his home. There he woke up his friend, General Henry Carrington and asked him to investigate to see what was going on. Together they walked the short distance to the Governor's House.

A second shot rang out but again it missed the two men. Carrington investigated the area but did not find the shooter. Morton believed that the Copperheads (Southern sympathizers in Indiana) were trying to kill him. Morton talked with the editor of the *Indianapolis Journal* and asked him not to print the story because he did not want to worry Lucinda. But the story leaked out.

# Chapter 15

# THE INCIDENT AT POGUE'S RUN

Another frightening incident took place on May 20, 1863. The Democrats were holding their state convention in Indianapolis with thousands in attendance, many from other states. It was rumored that a large number of Copperheads had come and that they were armed with many firearms. Morton had heard that the Knights of the Golden Circle, the secret society of those opposed to the war, were planning to overthrow the Indiana government. There were indications they might seek to assassinate him.

One report about the convention told of Union soldiers confronting and intimidating the attendees. During an afternoon session of the Democrat convention, eight or ten Union soldiers with bayonets fixed and guns cocked, entered the convention hall and moved toward the speaker's stand. Immediately, the crowd scattered, and the session quickly ended. Colonel John Coburn, who was in charge of the quartermaster's stores north of the Courthouse stopped the advancement of the soldiers into the hall.

Adding to the confusion, a squad of cavalry galloped near the building while the crowd scurried away. Toward the evening, some soldiers walked through the crowd and whenever negative remarks about the war or the Governor were heard, they arrested the offenders and threatened them. Most were let go, but several men were taken to the police station where about forty guns were taken from them.

When trains arrived for the Democrat delegates to leave Indianapolis, shots were heard coming from some railroad cars. The train on the Indiana Central Railroad was stopped. Policemen and soldiers entered the cars and demanded that all firearms be given up. About two hundred weapons were confiscated. Other trains were stopped and the Democrats threw their guns into the nearby creek. Reports of the number of weapons landing in the Pogue's Run creek were from 500 to 2,000. The term "Battle of Pogue's Run" was given by the Republicans who gloated over the outcome and praised the soldiers taking part. The Democrats called it a further assault on constitutional and civil rights by the supporters of Lincoln and Morton.

The constant military atmosphere of Indianapolis kept everyone on edge. Lucinda had more to worry about as the rumors of possible assassinations flew around Morton. It must have been a relief when the Democrat convention was over and the rumors settled down.

As the number of soldiers' casualties grew, more troops were needed at the front. With so many men leaving, Morton became concerned that Indiana did not have enough troops in the state to prevent a possible invasion. Confederate troops had already made attempts at invading Indiana but were repelled. His fears of invasion were confirmed in July 1863. Confederate Brigadier General John H. Morgan led his cavalry on a raid through Kentucky to divert Union General Ambrose Burnside's suspected plan to join Union Forces on an invasion of Tennessee. Morgan decided to go farther north into southern Indiana, thinking Southern sympathizers would join his regiment.

The war had taken a decisive turn for the Union army at the Battle of Vicksburg, Mississippi. On July 3, 1863, Lieutenant General John C. Pemberton surrendered his Confederate troops to General Ulysses

S. Grant after a siege of 47 days. One day later on July 4, one of the most deadly battles of the war came to an end at Gettysburg, Pennsylvania. On July 7, Indianapolis celebrated the victories with fireworks, speeches, and bonfires. The celebrations lasted only a short time as word came the next day that Morgan had crossed the Ohio River and invaded southern Indiana.

The word spread that Morgan intended to capture Indianapolis and to release and arm the rebel prisoners at Camp Morton. He was expected to tear up the railroads on his way to Indianapolis. Alarm bells rang in Indianapolis and large crowds gathered at the Bates House Hotel to hear speeches and the latest news. The following morning, July 9, Morton issued a proclamation asking Indianapolis business places to close at 3:00 that day.

The information about the coming raid filled the newspapers but was later shown to be unreliable. Confederate General Morgan had deliberately given out false information about his movements to confuse his enemies. He moved as fast as he could through several small towns in the southern part of the state.

While Indiana men were mustering to the latest cause, the women were joining the effort by preparing food and supplies for the Home

*Morgan's Raiders in southern Indiana.*

Guards (small groups of men organized to defend their towns) for the move against Morgan. Before the ill-prepared Home Guards could muster, Morgan's troops marched through southern Indiana, tearing up railroad tracks, burning depots and wooden water towers. They cut telegraph lines and burned train cars. The invaders had free rein in the unprepared towns to loot businesses and homes, taking money and valuables. Clothing, shoes, and food were favorite booty. In some towns he raided, Morgan demanded a ransom of $1,000 each from factories and mills to protect them against being burned. Most paid, because they had no choice if they wanted to save their property.

When the news of Morgan's Raid was made known, people all over the state were alarmed and ready to defend their homes. Governor Morton asked men who were not in the service to join their county militias and Home Guards to fight the invaders. An estimated 20,000 men arrived in Indianapolis to organize into military groups to fight Morgan's troops. The sounds of drums and fifes were again heard all over town as the men marched and drilled in the streets of Indianapolis. The Soldiers' Home was one of the places the men gathered. On one day, they fed 12,000 to 15,000 men.

The newly organized Indiana regiments and brigades were sent on trains to various points in southern Indiana and Ohio to fight Morgan. A frightening incident occurred as the recruits were preparing to leave. Just two blocks north of the State House, an artillery caisson (carriage for a cannon) accidentally exploded, killing a young boy, some soldiers, and a horse. This would have been very close to the Governor's House and his family. The whole neighborhood, including Lucinda's household, would have been frightened and expecting an attack. The rumors of Morgan's plan to release and arm the Confederate prisoners would have added to the panic that he was in the city and attacking it. Much to the relief of Indianapolis residents, it was a tragic accident and not an attack by Morgan.

Finally, after five days in Indiana, Morgan and his exhausted troops were routed and escaped into Ohio where they were chased down by

Brigadier General Edward Hobson and his force of over 3,000 men. Morgan was captured and put into prison, but he was later able to escape. Morgan's Raid had lasted three-and-a-half weeks, over 1,000 miles through Tennessee, Kentucky, Indiana, and Ohio. The raid had cost hundreds of thousands of dollars to the states in damages, both in military and civilian property. The people of Indiana were urged by Governor Morton to organize themselves into local militias to be prepared if another Confederate raid might threaten again.

# Chapter 16

# LADIES TO THE RESCUE

Inflation in prices of everyday goods and housing continued to rise, and crime increased on the streets of Indianapolis. Tired and lonely soldiers returning home to Indianapolis were easy prey for those who wanted to take advantage of them. Taverns were ordered not to sell liquor to soldiers, but they did anyway, and drunkenness was widespread. Wounded veterans, both in body and spirit, were scarred by the horrors of war that were hard to forget. The Soldiers' Home was a safe and welcoming place for soldiers to have meals and a bed when they stopped for a bit of rest.

Trains of wounded and furloughed soldiers arrived almost every day in Indianapolis. The local residents, as well as the representatives of the Sanitary Commission, welcomed them. Morton often met the trains himself and spoke to the returning troops. His show of sincere concern and the material support for Indiana's troops were greatly appreciated and he was given the name "The Soldiers' Friend."

Both Lucinda and Morton took time to visit the wounded in hospitals to see for themselves how the sick were cared for. They met the nurses and doctors and thanked them for their service. Lucinda worked with the Sanitary Commission and helped to bring in donations. When supplies were getting low, Lucinda would rally the ladies again. Many of the personal needs of soldiers on the field could not be purchased and the troops relied on the home front to help them.

*"Our Women and the War" by Homer Winslow, as it appeared in the September 2, 1862 edition of "Harper's Weekly."*

To emphasize the ongoing need for help, *The Richmond Palladium* published a letter on December 15, 1863, from Adjutant Oran Perry, of the 69th from Napo'eon (Napoleon), Arkansas, dated much earlier, January 17, 1863.) The letter was addressed "to our patriotic ladies, and we know they will respond without delay."

> *... One word in regard to our sanitary arrangements. Have all efforts ceased at home, except so far as physicians are concerned? I trust not; for you at home cannot imagine the comfort our poor fellows derive from something a little nice—prepared by the hands of our best friends at home, the women—God bless them! Nothing of the kind has arrived that I have heard of as yet—they may have at Nashville, but not reached here yet, where all our worst wounded are still in large numbers. Tell the good ladies of our town to push forward the noble work they have undertaken, and come themselves,*

*or send some trusty person with supplies, and see that their labors are not diverted from their proper use.*

The fight between the Union and the Confederacy was destroying the river town of Napoleon, Arkansas. Some of the Union soldiers with the worst wounds were taken to hospitals there. Although it was controlled by the Union, the town and troops lacked food and other necessities. The badly damaged town was eventually abandoned after floods and storms washed most of it into the Mississippi River.

Whenever Lucinda was aware that more help was needed, she picked up her pen to encourage patriotic women, again through newspaper articles, to help the suffering men. Lucinda's work with the Sanitary Commission and her ability to communicate with the public were great assets to the war effort. She did not hesitate to use her position as the Governor's wife, to set an example and to encourage the women of the state to keep up their good work.

Early in 1864, a call went out for more solders. The Union troops were battle weary, many had died or were permanently disabled, and some had completed their term of enlistment and wanted to come home. Men were needed to fill the ranks. Prior to this, when troops were needed, they had been drafted, which was very unpopular. A bounty for payment was offered for men to enlist or reenlist. On April 6, 1864, General William Tecumseh Sherman sent a telegram to Governor Morton to recruit all the men he could. "Three hundred men in time," he said, "were better than a thousand too late. Every soldier should be at his place in the front."

The urgent plea set Morton's creative mind into devising a plan to help. He suggested troops be enlisted for 100 days. Morton conferred with the Governors of Ohio, Illinois, Wisconsin, and Iowa at a meeting in Indianapolis. Although many other plans were suggested, it was Morton's idea that was agreed upon. The governors proposed to the President that these states furnish eighty-five thousand troops for one hundred days. Lincoln approved it.

As much as possible, these men would come from those who stayed at home to operate businesses or other essential jobs and farms. How could the home front keep up if the men left their jobs? Immediately, a plan was suggested to the Ladies' Patriotic Association. Mrs. Morton placed this announcement in the newspapers on April 26.

**20,000 Lady Volunteers**

**LADIES TO THE RESCUE!!**

**Twenty thousand additional troops for 100 days have been called for. Many of our patriotic ladies feeling their services may, at this time when all are called on to interest themselves, and do something, be of use to the struggling country, have determined to volunteer in the service by taking the places of the gentlemen who would cheerfully go, but whose business *cannot*, be suspended – They cannot fill the place of all, but can relieve many who would go. They propose that all ladies who are earnestly solicitous of promoting our country's interest meet at Masonic Hall tomorrow (Wednesday) at 2 ½ o'clock P M when the matter will be fully presented and the books opened for enlistments. Let it be said of each one, "she hath done what she could."**

**Mrs. O P MORTON**

**L. P. Association**

**G. Newman, Sec'y**

The next day, there was a large gathering of ladies at the Masonic Hall in Indianapolis. The meeting was called to order by Colonel James Blake. He explained that the purpose of the call was to determine how many ladies would be willing to volunteer to take the places of men who would enlist from Indianapolis. The women were not expected to go to war, but to fill the men's jobs while they were gone. Blake stated that the ladies had more power in this country than the President himself. If the ladies did not stand by the President, he could not carry on the war for an hour.

After his flowery salute to women, he introduced Mrs. Governor Morton who would preside over the meeting. Lucinda was described as presiding neatly, elegantly, and like a true, noble, and patriotic speaker. She thanked everyone for the honor conferred and the purpose of the meeting was addressed. It was to procure ladies to take the place of gentlemen and conduct their business while they were in the service of their country. She then introduced Mrs. Canfield, the widow of a gallant Ohio officer who gave his life for his country on the bloody field of Shiloh.

Mrs. Canfield was passing through Indianapolis when she heard about Morton's call for enlistments of 100 days. Because of her own work at some of the battlefields, it was her suggestion that women be employed to help fill the men's jobs while they were gone. Her suggestions included how it would be done, how the women would be paid—soldier's pay at $13 a month—with the men continuing to be paid their salaries during their service, and that their jobs be reinstated when they came home. Mrs. Canfield had contacted Mrs. Morton and related her ideas. Mrs. Morton and others of the Ladies' Patriotic Association agreed that this was a good plan.

The women attending the meeting responded enthusiastically to Mrs. Canfield's plan and Lucinda's enthusiasm for it. Many volunteers signed up that day. In the next few days, women of the Ladies' Patriotic Association were assigned to certain sections of the business community in Indianapolis to contact and get support for hiring women to take the places of the men who planned to volunteer—except for the saloons!

According to the *Indianapolis Sentinel's* account of the Association's effort, "they were almost everywhere received with courtesy and kindness, and met with good success, the businessmen generally sympathizing in the cause which led to so novel a movement."

Soliciting the help of businessmen willing to hire women also caused these business owners to encourage their male employees to volunteer for the army.

In short order, women took over jobs that were traditionally men's and performed them well. Not everyone approved of the women taking jobs in business. As soon as information about the project was reported in the newspapers, critics made their feelings known. This sarcastic ad in the *Sentinel* appeared on April 29.

> *Wanted—Two ladies who can produce certificates of good moral character, to take the places of the proprietor and his clerk in No. 1 saloon, so that they can go to war. Address P. O. Box 1714. Everything strictly confidential.*

It was rare for women to be employed in professional or business places to serve the public, although women did help in family owned stores and business. The war changed the situation for women to be able to earn money in a traditional man's job. Women were serving as nurses and helpers with the sick and wounded, but nursing was not considered the same as "man's" work. However, their service was not only critical for the health of soldiers but was a much-needed element for keeping up the morale of the wounded.

Women and girls in the New England states had been employed in textile mills since the 1820s. Lowell, Massachusetts built textile factories and enticed young women from the poor farming families to come to the city to work in the mills. This was behind-the-scenes work where women were not exposed to the public. The pay was low and the working conditions harsh, and by 1843, nearly 30,000 women were employed. Although this had allowed women to earn a living, it created such a difficult environment that the workers carried out strikes and petitioned politicians to pass a law to limit the number of working hours in a day. It took many years before women workers would receive pay equal to men and for working conditions to improve. Factory work was one thing, but a woman working outside the home to serve the public in business places was unheard of in most states.

The call for the enlistments of 100 days gave women the opportunity to show their ability to work in occupations traditionally filled by men. Most of the new short-term female work force was made up of young, unmarried women who had attended school. Many of the young women were well educated, although that was not a requirement. Shopkeepers found that young women could keep books, act as secretaries, handle and sell the goods as well as men. School committees found that young women could conduct schools throughout the year as well as a man. The telegraph company, after hiring women, found that they could receive and send telegrams accurately and efficiently. The necessity of women stepping into the workforce opened the door, so that after the war, it was no longer unacceptable for a woman to earn her own living in professions that were usually held by men. Lucinda Morton led the movement in Indianapolis to help women gain this opportunity.

Reacting to the increasing taxes and a raise in tariffs for imported goods in early 1864, the wives of members of Lincoln's Cabinet and of Senators and Representatives, as well as other ladies of standing, decided to do something about it. Their mission was to encourage women of the Union states to stop buying imported clothing and accessories. The trade deficit with other countries was wrecking the American economy. The money sent overseas for goods was needed at home by the enormous cost of the war.

The dress style of women in the 1860s was the crinoline or hooped skirt. The crinoline was made of a stiff fabric with cotton or linen dress lining. This allowed the lady's overskirt to spread full and wide. The style was extremely popular among women of all social standing and class in the Western world, first becoming popular in the 1850s. The more expensive the dress, the wider the hoop became until it was very difficult to negotiate through doors, to ride in a carriage, or sit on a chair. As a necessity, the extreme size of the hoops of the 1850s began to evolve into a flatter front in the mid-1860s, with most of the fullness toward the back of the dress. The wide skirts and elaborate bodices of a dress required as much as 12 to 14 yards of material. Only the wealthy could afford such expensive fashions.

On May 14, the *Evansville Daily Journal* and other newspapers printed an article describing the first meeting in Washington, D.C., of the women who were organizing the Ladies' National Covenant, sometimes called the Ladies' Loyal League. Their mission was to encourage women not to purchase imported clothing and material, but to keep the money at home. 'Buy American' was the theme. American-made clothing material was scarce and expensive as most of it went into supplies and clothing for the war. The Ladies' National Covenant pledged to buy American whenever possible, and only when it could not be provided would they buy imported goods.

Women representing Union states attended the meeting in Washington. Mrs. Joanna Lane (Former Indiana Governor Henry Lane's wife) was one of the organizers. An advisory committee of five women from each state was appointed. Lucinda Morton was selected for Indianapolis and took part in the Washington meeting. Patriotism was the theme, and women were asked to take a pledge to buy American products. A national badge was created for a woman to wear to show that she had taken the pledge. The badge was a black bee pin on the national colors. Even if a person had to wear her imported dresses, she could wear her pin, and everyone would know that she would buy American when she could. Lucinda was willing to take up any patriotic cause that would help the country.

*Reproduction of the American Bee banner.*

# Chapter 17

# THE HOME FRONT AND THE ELECTION OF 1864

One of the prominent issues was the coming election for Indiana Governor in 1864. The war had been at a low mark in early 1863. But the tide seemed to be turning for the Union side with the battle of Gettysburg in July 1863. There was still a long way to go and Morton was constantly at odds with state officials. He had made many personal enemies. The Democrats had control of the State Legislature and they and the Peace Republicans worked to undermine him. According to historian Logan Esarey in his *A History of Indiana*, this was his description of Morton, "he belabored his opponents until they went down bruised and sore. He was the embodiment of the war, stalwart, blunt, and soldierly."

Despite Morton's strong and often disputed control of the state's affairs, he was still seen by many as doing his best for the soldiers and the state. When it came to electing the Governor for 1864, the majority of Indiana residents saw no one but Morton to continue to lead, and he won the election.

There was little time at home for Morton family life. Morton spent long hours at the State House and traveled to see for himself what was happening with the war. Besides his travels, Morton made many speeches for his reelection during the summer.

Although the Governor kept a strenuous schedule of work, speeches, and his frequent travels, he was described as a loving husband and father. He discussed his speeches and probably the latest events and decisions with Lucinda. He spared her as much as he could from details that would distress her. Morton was fond of his boys, and Lucinda brought them to Morton's office to see him when he was too busy to spend time at home. According to his funeral eulogy, he always greeted them with a kiss.

When their oldest son, John, finished school at White Water College in Centerville, he had enrolled in Earlham College in Richmond in the fall of 1863. When the boys visited in Centerville, they stayed with grandparents or other relatives who lived there. Lucinda rarely traveled with Morton at this time. The children, the number of guests visiting the Governor's House, and the work of the Ladies' Patriotic Society consumed most of her time.

Lucinda had married a strong man, both in body and mind. He had a strong work ethic and a strong will. Morton could be abrasive and blunt to his enemies but also was described as being outgoing, friendly, and loyal to his friends. Lucinda in many ways was his opposite. Morton trusted her and willingly turned over personal and family affairs to her. Lucinda was not a clinging vine, nor did she try to "manage" him. Where Morton was strong, passionate, and outspoken, Lucinda was tactful and gracious, no doubt many times smoothing over irritated feelings of others. She was intelligent, industrious, and strong in her faith and attitudes. She had a strong will, but it was exercised in terms of the work needing to be done.

In spite of the war, many improvements had come to the Indiana home by the late 1860s. Coal was readily available for heating and cooking. Any room that was not used daily was not heated in winter. The warmest room was the kitchen. When guests were expected, the sitting room or dining area was heated by a fireplace or stove. Most bedrooms were not heated in winter unless someone was ill or of old age. Bedrooms on the upper floors were heated by registers in the floor over a stove. Some bedrooms might have a fireplace. Gas was becoming more available, mostly for lighting. Some improvements were made to the Governor's House, but they could not cover up its deficiencies.

As progress grew with new factories and business in Indiana created by the war effort, it produced new wealth. Farm products were much in demand. Businesses who catered to the war effort also thrived. But soldiers' families suffered loss of income from their men serving in the military, and many became destitute. Soldiers' pay was small and most of them tried to send it home. Mail was not dependable and the money was not always paid on time or able to reach the family. The contrast was great between the poor and the wealthy. However, the new prosperity for some helped create and introduce new products and jobs, and overall raised the standard of living.

Money was always needed to help the soldiers and their families. Aid societies, churches, and communities throughout Indiana held sanitary fairs, suppers, and entertainments to raise funds. People were generous and enjoyed the times of fellowship and working together.

In August 1864, a call was made for the patriotic women of Indianapolis to plan a series of entertainments in connection with the Sanitary Fair. It was planned to be at the same time as the State Fair. A meeting to prepare for it was held at the residence of Mrs. Governor Morton in the afternoon at four o'clock. Lucinda helped organize and set up committees for the extravagant Sanitary Fair.

The Indiana State Fair and the Sanitary Fair were held from October 3–8. Special rates were given to people coming on trains. One Indianapolis reporter described his trip to the Fairgrounds. "We yesterday, paying five cents, took the street railroad cars, propelled hydraulically by bob-tailed mules, and got within two squares of the gates.... We saw Power Hall; we saw Floral Hall; we saw Miscellaneous Hall; we saw the giant; we saw the fat woman; we saw a monkey and fed it crackers ...We saw Sanitary Hall along side

*Sanitary Fair in 1864.*

of a windmill … We saw the whole of the institution so far as it has progressed, and we used our legs to bring ourselves back into the city with a determined purpose to go out there again, probably today."

Banner awards were given to the two counties that contributed the most to the Sanitary Fair. The first banner went to Vanderburgh County for the contributions from Evansville. The second banner went to little Union County. *The New York Times* on October 21, 1864 reported that the Indiana Sanitary Fair had brought in $40,000. This would go for the work of the Indiana Sanitary Commission.

Evansville, Vanderburgh County, was awarded its beautiful banner a short time later. Chaplain John Lozier presented it. Lozier was very involved in caring for the helpless soldiers, their widows, and orphans and served as Chaplain on the battlefield for the 37th Indiana. Later, he became the financial agent for the Soldiers' Home. In 1864, he published a song honoring Governor Morton, "Cottage of the Dear Ones Left at Home," words by John Hogarth Lozier, music by J. H. Butterfield. There were at least three songs published that honored

Governor Morton. His picture was on the fronts of the sheet music.

Governor Morton had another disturbing challenge in the summer and fall of 1864. He was already busy with war issues and the coming election for Governor. His problems and concerns escalated with the Democrats and the Southern sympathizers' organizations generally known as the Copperheads. Almost from the beginning of the war, these secret groups did all they could to disrupt the Indiana war effort and threaten the Governor. With the help of agents secretly joining the various organizations and frequent reporting to Morton, the authorities were able to arrest and charge the ringleaders with conspiracy and treason. The sensational trials were a distraction for the population and politicians.

In the fall of 1864, Oliver P. Morton won the election for Indiana Governor and Abraham Lincoln was reelected as President. This gave Morton some relief from the stress of the campaign. The treason trials of the Copperheads basically put an end to the secret organizations of Southern sympathizers. Many of the defendants were found guilty and some executed.

## Moving From The Governor's House

The dilapidated Governor's House had become too much of a problem for Lucinda. The family and staff had often been ill during the couple of years they lived there. Lucinda believed their health problems were because of the poor condition of the house. It was not worth the money for the government to repair it, and it was time to move.

In early December 1864, it was reported that the Governor's family had moved out of the Governor's House and that the legislature was trying to decide what to do with the property. According to the *Evansville Daily Journal* in February 1866, "The Governor's House had become so dilapidated that it was utterly unfit for occupancy …"

The property was situated close to the State House and because business property in that area was in demand, the house and grounds were sold for $41,000. Until a suitable residence was purchased or built for the use of the Governor, Morton would be allowed up to $5,000 per year to rent a place. According to Lucinda, they moved for a time into the Bates House Hotel, which was a short distance from the Governor's House and the State House. The hotel had large rooms that could accommodate receptions and social affairs of the Governor. The hotel was lighted by gas and had installed bathrooms as early as 1853.

Sarah Burbank had lived with her sister, Lucinda, and helped with the care of the Governor's House. She moved home to live with her parents in Centerville after the Mortons moved into the Bates House Hotel. On March 27, 1865, she married First Lieutenant Caleb B. Gill. He served in the 57th Regiment Indiana Volunteers and resigned on May 7, 1865, after being promoted to Captain. He died in 1867, leaving his wife and baby daughter.

The war was winding down in the spring of 1865. Although the Union was winning, the horrific cost of life on both sides was still going on. The War Between the States effectively came to the end on April 9, 1865, when Confederate General Robert E. Lee surrendered to Union General Ulysses S. Grant at Appomattox Court House in Virginia. It was good news for the nation, although this was only the first of the Confederate armies to surrender. Battles continued, but soon the remainder of the Confederate army began to fall like dominoes. It was not until August 1866 that President Andrew Johnson declared that the war officially ended.

# *Chapter 18*

# CELEBRATION AND MOURNING

Indiana began to feel optimistic that the war was ending and the soldiers would be coming home. There was great rejoicing in the cities such as Richmond, Indiana. The *Richmond Palladium,* April 14, reported that wood was piled up, making "the largest fires ever before seen in our Quaker City." There were speeches, music, fireworks, and the crowds noisily rejoicing.

The Morton household was awakened early on the morning of April 15, when a telegram arrived telling of the attack on President Lincoln and that he was not expected to live. He died that day, April 15, 1865. The whole nation was thrown into shock. What

**ASSASSINATION OF THE PRESIDENT.**

**ATTEMPTED MURDER OF SECRETARY SEWARD AND SONS.**

**Despatches from Secretary Stanton.**

WAR DEPARTMENT,
WASHINGTON, D. C., April 15—1.30 P. M.

*Major General John A. Dix, New York:*

Last evening, at 10.30 p. m., at Ford's Theater, the President, while sitting in his private box with Mrs. Lincoln, Miss Harris, and Maj. Rathbun, was shot by an assassin who suddenly entered the box. He approached behind the President. The assassin then leaped upon the stage, brandishing a large dagger or knife, and made his escape by the rear of the theater. The pistol ball entered the back of the President's head. The wound is mortal. The President has been insensible ever since it was inflicted, and is now dying.

About the same hour an assassin, either the same or another, entered Mr. Seward's house, and, under pretence of having a prescription, was shown to the Secretary's sick chamber. The Secretary was in bed, a nurse and Miss Seward with him. The assassin immediately rushed to the bed, inflicting two or three stabs on the throat, and two in the face. It is hoped the wounds may not be mortal. My apprehension is that they will prove fatal. The nurse alarmed Mr. Frederick Seward, who was in an adjoining room, and hastened to the door of his father's room, where he met the assassin, who inflicted upon him one or more dangerous wounds. The recovery of Frederick Seward is doubtful.

*A newspaper article reporting the assassination of President Lincoln.*

had begun with thanksgiving and celebration turned into despair and mourning. Governor Morton was a close friend of Lincoln and frequently traveled to Washington to consult with him. Morton called for the city and state to take down the celebration decorations and gather to mourn the fallen President.

Calvin Fletcher of Indianapolis, who kept diaries from 1817 to 1866, recorded his shock at receiving the news about Lincoln's assassination. "… One of the most appalling announcements except the announcement of the sudden death of my poor son Miles in 1862 that has ever been made to me." It was Mr. Fletcher's son that was killed on the supply train with Morton and companions in Sullivan, Indiana.

Fletcher's thoughts and feelings reflected how the nation felt. Even Lincoln's political opponents in the north were shocked and appalled at what happened. They quickly declared their loyalty and disassociated themselves from such a terrible deed.

President Lincoln's final interment was to be in Springfield, Illinois. A funeral train was prepared in Washington to carry him and his son Willie, who had died in the White House in 1862, to their burial place. Mrs. Lincoln was in shock and too ill to take the train or attend the funeral. The nine-car train left Washington escorted by several dignitaries, friends, and family. About 150 were invited to travel with the body. Governor Morton had been invited, but he remained in Indianapolis. He and other dignitaries would join the train when it entered Indiana.

The train left Washington on April 21, traveling the same route in reverse, as his inaugural train trip in 1861. It arrived in Richmond on April 30 about 3:00 a.m. Governor Morton and party boarded the train there for the trip back to Indianapolis. Crowds of people lined the train tracks all along the way. Every town, large or small, prepared special tributes as the funeral train passed through. It reached Indianapolis at 7:00 a.m. where quiet crowds, soldiers, and officials met it. They had been patiently waiting in the pouring rain.

According to the *Indianapolis Daily Gazette*, "the archways and mourning festoons across the streets, the public and private buildings draped in the habiliments of grief, the funeral procession, the solemn dirges, and above all, the patient multitude that stood for hours in the drenching rain waiting an opportunity to look upon the earthly tenement so lately vacated by the spirit …"

The casket moved to the State House, passing through crowds of people lining the streets. The State House had been prepared and decorated inside and out. Some people who had traveled the whole route from Washington stated that the decorations and programming in Indianapolis were the best they had seen in any state along the way.

The casket was placed in the rotunda of the State House and was ready for viewing at 9:00 a.m. Tickets were given to VIPs for a special time to view the body. The first to enter the rotunda were groups of Sunday school children and ladies. They entered four abreast and were divided so that there were two passing on each side of the casket. Honor guards kept the people moving as rapidly as possible so that everyone who came would have a chance to see Lincoln in his casket.

An outdoor program had been planned, but the rain was constant and the streets turned to mud. The viewing hours in the rotunda lasted until 10:00 p.m., longer than planned, but allowing for more people to come through. The body was taken back to the train, where it resumed its journey to Springfield, Illinois. Morton sent a group representing Indiana on the train to attend the funeral. Among them were William Holloway his secretary, and his son, John M. Morton. Although Lucinda must have attended the service in the rotunda and the viewing, there was no mention of any women, except in general—women with children in their arms and ladies with the Sunday school children.

After the Lincoln Funeral Train went on its way, Indianapolis moved quickly back to the problems caused by the ending of the war. On May 1, the next day, four companies of the 63$^{rd}$ Regiment and the 23$^{rd}$ Army Corps arrived in Indianapolis to be mustered out. The ladies prepared a hearty breakfast at the Soldiers' Home. The soldiers marched to the State House where Morton gave a speech welcoming them, thanking them, and praising them for their service. He spoke about issues still facing the country as it recovered. Thus began a grueling schedule for Morton as he tried to meet as many of the returning soldiers as he could.

There were many difficulties for the returning soldiers and their families that needed to be addressed. Morton, Lucinda, and his staff worked to establish a Children's Home in Knightstown for orphans of veterans. The cemetery at Crown Hill was still being developed. Ill and wounded returning soldiers needed medical care. Many families were still destitute and somehow they must have help. So many new issues arose with the returning soldiers. Morton also was involved in trying to help with the reconstruction plan for the country, often consulting with President Johnson.

It was obvious to his wife and others that Morton was ill during the summer of 1865. He tried to continue attending receptions for the soldiers as they came through Indianapolis. Meeting the almost daily receptions for the veterans was too much for him, and he showed his fatigue by barely being able to attend. Morton's biographer, William Dudley Foulke, describes him as "so haggard and careworn that he could hardly deliver the speech of welcome expected of him, and sometimes had to stay away."

By early August, Morton had to admit to himself and others that he needed a break from the stress. He traveled to Niagara Falls to get away and rest. In his letter to Lucinda he describes his relief.

*My Dear Wife,*

*I reached here Friday night feeling better than I have done for many weeks. Yesterday and today I have been entirely free from pain in my back, and can hardly realize the sudden relief on account of it. The atmosphere is very bracing, soft moist breeze from the falls is delightful, and the place is as charming as ever, but I am lonesome ... I have two dispatches saying Ollie (their youngest son) is better. The news was very grateful to me, and I am impatient to see him and his dear mother."*

The short vacation helped Morton revive his strength and enthusiasm. When he came home, he insisted on resuming his busy schedule, against the advice of his personal physician and the concern of his family. His health again began to deteriorate, but he refused to slow down.

The need for the Indiana State Sanitary Commission was coming to an end. A prize banner was awarded to the county contributing the largest sum to the commission for the relief of sick and wounded soldiers in the year 1864. Wayne County, Morton's birthplace, had won the banner, and a celebration was planned for its presentation. On September 29, 1865, the celebration was held in Richmond for the award, and Morton gave a lengthy speech focusing on the question of reconstruction for the nation. This was Morton's last public address before his stroke.

## Morton Stricken With Paralysis

Morton realized he had been forgetting things and becoming confused, and everything seemed more difficult. He had lost interest in reading and keeping up with the news, and he was more tired than usual. Just a few days after his speech in Richmond, he paid the price for his overwork. On October 10, 1865, he woke up in the morning and read the morning newspaper while still in bed. When he tried to get up, he found that he was unable to move his legs. He had suffered a stroke. Other members of his family had experienced similar problems. Morton's father was a paralytic in his later years and one of his aunts had a similar affliction.

Morton's physician diagnosed it as "paralysis perophliga," a general term describing paralysis. Strokes can be caused by several factors, but many are caused by high blood pressure and heart arrhythmia. Lucinda, no doubt, was very worried that her husband was so ill and perhaps might not live. There was little to be done for him but rest. Medicine had improved greatly during the Civil War, but the effects of a stroke and medicines to treat it were still lacking.

Lucinda's life changed as dramatically as her husband's. She had to assume the burden of all the family affairs as well as help Morton recover. She lost her strong, energetic husband and realized that he would probably never be physically strong again. They might never be able to be intimate again. It was difficult and saddening to see him a broken and crippled man, barely able to get around.

After a few weeks, Morton slowly began to recover, but his legs were still paralyzed. From this time on, he was never able to stand without the aid of crutches or a cane. He had to sit to give speeches. But he recovered enough to consider seeking medical treatment in France. He was willing to step down from being Governor and let the Lieutenant Governor handle things for a time.

Morton spoke to the State Legislature in November, hardly a month after he was struck down. He made a speech outlining his concerns and apologized for having to sit. He made his leave of absence official and turned the Governor's duties over to Lieutenant Governor Conrad Baker. Dr. W. C. Thompson, Morton's physician, had been very concerned about him for several months. He spoke to the State Legislature at this time about Morton's condition, to assure them he had done all he could to prevent it.

"I earnestly recommended his withdrawal from the cares of office as early as the first of September.... I was unable to prevail upon him to withdraw from the duties of his office at that time. He thought it necessary to give his personal attention to the management of the public business and interests of the state. But I never ceased to admonish him of the danger of so doing."

Oliver had recovered somewhat but still had paralysis in his legs.

He consulted with other doctors with no new help. Some new methods for treating his condition were being used in Europe, and he decided to make the trip to try to fully recover.

## A Trip to Europe

Asserting his strong will, although still not well, Morton began his trip by traveling to Washington for a week before he started his trip to Europe. He conferred with President Johnson, who asked him to deliver a message to Louis Napoleon Bonaparte, also known as Napoleon III, Emperor of France. The goal of this secret mission was to persuade Napoleon to remove French troops from Mexico.

The trip to Europe and his treatment in Paris would be expensive. Since Morton would also be undertaking a government mission, he was given financial aid for his trip. Secretary of War Edwin Stanton sent a doctor with him to oversee his health and treatment. Stanton's instructions to Morton stated, "To defray your necessary expenses in performing these duties, a reasonable compensation, fixed by the President, will be allowed."

Lucinda remained in Indianapolis to settle the home affairs and make arrangements for their sons. The younger boys stayed in Centerville with the Burbank family. Their older son, John, had been attending Earlham College in Richmond. He left the school to travel with his parents to Europe. John did not return to Earlham but finished his education later at the North Western Christian University in Indianapolis.

Lucinda, John, and Morton's former private secretary, Berry Sulgrove, met Morton in New York where they boarded the ship, the *Scotia*. The captain graciously turned over his cabin to Morton and Lucinda for their comfort. The ship docked in Liverpool, England, and the small party spent the Christmas holidays there. They traveled to France where Morton was to receive treatment for his paralysis.

In January 1866, Morton met with Napoleon III to deliver the President's request to remove his troops and influence from Mexico. The meeting was successful and Napoleon III agreed. At the close of their meeting, Napoleon III invited Morton and Lucinda to a formal reception at the Tuileries Palace. Morton planned to attend, but he decided it would be too much of an ordeal due to his health. Lucinda represented him by attending the reception in the company of several other American dignitaries and their ladies.

*Tuileries Palace, Paris, circa 1865. The royal palace of Louis Napoleon Bonaparte, Emperor of France from 1852–1870. Louis Napoleon Bonaparte was the nephew of Napoleon Bonaparte.*

Lucinda's gown for the reception was described in the American newspapers. The *Marshall County Republican*, Plymouth, Indiana reported, "Mrs. Gov. Morton of Indiana wore a rich mauve colored satin, with pearl trimming, white lace, and a diamond rosette in her hair."

Attending a reception at the palace of the Emperor of France called for the finest gowns that one could afford. Empress Eugenia's favorite dress designer was Charles Frederick Worth. It was the "thing" for a wealthy American lady visiting France in the 1860s to purchase a gown from the House of Worth. The description of Lucinda's gown suggests that it may have been purchased from this prestigious dress salon, if they could have afforded it.

By the time Lucinda visited Paris in 1866, Worth had been changing his designs from the increasingly wide hoop skirt to making women's skirts narrower and a flatter front with more of the material at the back. This led to the bustle style of the 1870–1880s. His innovative designs became very popular and were featured in American magazines such as *Godey's Lady's Book*.

Governor and Mrs. Morton's movements were followed closely on their trip by their champions and their critics. The news was sent by telegram. The *Richmond Palladium* reported that the Julian "organ" (Isaac Julian's newspaper that had moved to Richmond) "recently exceeded itself in the abuse of Governor Morton, by a cowardly and contemptible paragraph relating to Mrs. Morton's dress at the French Court. The organ with its jackal propensities, picked up the putrid bone and handed it around to its readers as a delectable morsel."

The article in the paper accused Governor Morton of having stolen a great deal of money from the people of the state so his wife could have the expensive clothing. However, Morton's financial affairs relating to the war had been carefully recorded and accounted for. There was no federal or state money stolen by Morton or those who handled the war finances.

A few days after the reception at the Tuileries, Morton went for treatment to the somewhat controversial, but popular physician, Charles-Édouard Brown-Séquard in Paris. Morton's condition is now recognized as Brown-Séquard Syndrome, a rare neurological condition characterized by a lesion in the spinal cord, which results in weakness or paralysis on one side of the body and a loss of sensation on the opposite side. It may be caused by a tumor, or some kind of damage to the spinal cord. Morton's doctors stated that he had fallen earlier on his left side, where the paralysis settled. His right side was affected by the loss of sensation. The treatment was the Eastern "moxa," that seemed to have helped others with a similar condition.

While getting ready for the treatment, Morton asked his friend Sulgrove to attend the treatment and to be ready to help him if he needed it. Sulgrove "begged off," knowing Lucinda would be with him. He confessed that he couldn't bear to see him suffer under the torture of cautery, of burning with a white-hot iron.

The treatment was not by cautery of a hot iron, but by caustic potash applied in two places close to the backbone. Cautery with a hot iron would have taken about a minute, while the potash burning took about eight minutes. The process was described, "It ate two holes in the back, one on each side of the spinal column, and each big enough for a man's finger. It was more painful because it was more protracted than burning with a hot iron."

Both ether and chloroform were available as anesthetics. Morton was given medication, but there was still a lot of pain for him. He was not one to complain, but soon it became clear that the treatment was not going to help him as it had helped others. Lucinda stayed by his side through the treatment, and no doubt, was much distressed at his suffering. The painful ordeal did little to help him.

Morton had intended to spend more time in other European countries, but his condition was such that he only stayed a short time longer. His son John returned home before them in February. President Johnson had wanted Morton to do some other things in Europe, but he decided it was time to get back to his job as Governor.

## Back Home Again

Lucinda and Morton boarded a ship for home, parting ways with Sulgrove. The voyage was much different than the trip over. The seas were rougher and the bulwarks were crushed with large waves. A fire broke out and the ship was in danger of destruction. Finally, the ship arrived safely in New York. They stayed there for a time where Morton met with a Republican Senator. Doctors examined him in New York, and although his condition seemed improved, paralysis would always affect his ability to walk without some kind of support.

While Morton was resuming his connections with the political situation, Lucinda visited friends. A newspaper account told of her receiving a gift of a silver tea service from friends in New York. After a trip to Washington for Morton to meet with President Johnson, Lucinda and her husband arrived back in Indianapolis on April 12, 1866.

The Morton family had lived for a time at the Bates House Hotel. They moved to a rented house and then purchased a nice residence on the southeast corner of New York Street and Pennsylvania Street. The address was 149 North Pennsylvania Street. It was a large double house that would accommodate the family and guests, with rooms that could be opened together for entertaining.

Morton took over the Governor's position and found the Republicans discouraged and demoralized because of President Johnson's policies. He worked to encourage them and to shut down his enemies. Although Morton was never able to recover physical strength in his legs, his mind was as sharp as ever. He did not accept defeat and made important speeches to rally the Republicans in the state.

When Morton left for Europe, his many friends wished him a full recovery. Even some of the Indiana Democrats had put aside politics and expressed their good wishes for him. But upon his return, the old enemies and critics renewed their attacks with even more harsh accusations and lies. Democrat newspapers printed rumors and made up their own vile attacks.

After the Mortons came home from Europe, rumors and innuendos were circulated by his enemies that he had not made the trip to Europe for his paralysis, but that he was being treated for a venereal disease. His doctors, family, and friends who were with him on this difficult and painful trip quickly discounted the lies.

It was nearing election time and Morton was not eligible to run again for Indiana Governor. On January 2, 1867, the Indiana Legislature met to elect a man to replace Senator Henry Lane. Morton won against his Democratic opponent.

Lieutenant Governor Baker again assumed the office of Governor and ran against the Democratic nominee, Thomas A. Hendricks. Baker was elected in 1868.

Lucinda would be filling a new role with her husband as Mrs. Senator Morton.

# Part 3

## MRS. SENATOR MORTON

# Chapter 19

# THE MORTONS GO TO WASHINGTON

Life changed rapidly for the Morton family in 1867, when Oliver P. Morton was elected to the U.S. Senate. Lieutenant Governor Conrad Baker then became the Indiana Governor. The Mortons prepared to give up their new residence, according to *The Evansville Journal.* On February 5, 1867, the newspaper stated, "Governor Baker will occupy the residence now occupied by Senator Morton." The house was not sold, but rented to Governor Baker.

Senator Morton left for Washington on February 12, 1867. He took his seat in the Senate on March 4. Lucinda arranged to move their household, possibly leaving some furnishings for the Baker family. They would still need a home in Indianapolis for their sons and when the Senate was not in session, and may have rented another place. Their son John, 21, was in school in Indianapolis at North Western Christian University. Walter, 11, and Oliver T. (Ollie), 7, would likely stay with family in Centerville while attending the school sessions at the Centerville Collegiate Institute. The school was still in the buildings of the Wayne County Seminary, but had changed administrations and ownerships over the years. The school offered elementary to collegiate level classes for male and female students. The same high standards of the school had continued. When new state school laws were passed, circa 1870, the institution was converted to the Centerville public school.

Lucinda found the Washington social climate very different from Indianapolis. She had become the leader of society in Indianapolis while she was the wife of the Governor. As a U.S. Senator's wife, she had to take on a lesser social role in the nation's capital. The rigid Washington City social life and protocol had been established and maintained from the earliest days when it was designated the nation's capital. Lucinda had visited Washington many times and was acquainted with women who lived there. Mrs. Joanna Lane was the wife of the former Indiana Senator Henry Lane, whom Morton was replacing. Mrs. Lane would have been able to advise Lucinda as she prepared to follow the Washington social rules.

*A Matthew Brady photo of Washington, D.C. in May of 1865, just after the end of the Civil War and about two years before the Mortons moved there.*

Lucinda was no stranger to high society social behavior. She had made friends in England and Europe when they went to France for Morton's paralysis treatment in 1865. When an invitation came to them for a reception at the royal palace, Lucinda attended without

Morton, as his health did not permit it. She was accompanied by other American diplomats and friends. The reception at the French palace demanded the strictest social etiquette and the finest of dress. Because of these experiences, Lucinda would have been prepared to handle high society in Washington, D.C.

U.S. Senators and Representatives usually lived in Washington hotels or boarding houses near the Capitol buildings during the legislative sessions. Morton moved into rooms in the National Hotel. He could walk with his crutches to the hotel's entrance and then be taken by cab or carriage to the Senate building. As much as possible, Morton tried to ignore his disability and continued to attend to his

*A photograph of Senator Oliver Morton taken by Matthew Brady.*

senatorial duties. At various times, he wrote to Lucinda of the day's activities and spoke of feeling too "feeble" to carry out his planned agenda.

In the nation's capital, social standing was determined by official rank. The President was regarded as the First Man in the nation's society status, as well as being the President. His office was open to receive calls, mostly in the morning, when he had no other official business meetings. A visitor presented a calling card, and according to his business with the President, was shown into his office.

Calling cards were important for business as well as for social calls. Neither the President nor his wife was expected to return calls. For others in Washington, the calling card etiquette required a return visit. There were many rules about making calls, using calling cards, acknowledging the calls, and returning them. It was the duty of the politician's wife or his secretary's task to be sure the rules were followed. When Lucinda was in Washington, she was expected to follow the strict rules of visiting. Wives of politicians were kept busy following the rules, giving receptions, teas, or dinners, and keeping up the proper social contacts. According to the 1883 book of *American Etiquette and Rules of Politeness*, it was stated that, "A clever woman, whom we met making a round of receptions and visits last winter (in Washington), said to us, 'You do not see my chain, but I am a galley slave none the less.' She was speaking of the senseless waste of time involved in the treadmill of social visits," according to this book on Washington etiquette.

The rules of entertaining were also important. The President and his wife were expected to give receptions and other social events. One did not turn down an invitation from the President. It was also the duty of Cabinet members to entertain. But for Senators and Representatives, entertaining was optional. However, it was important to politicians that the wives and family keep in close contact with each other. Social relations were kept as friendly as possible even though the politicians might not agree when at work.

President Andrew Johnson became President at the death of Abraham Lincoln, April 15, 1865. He was a Tennessee Democrat, but after Tennessee joined the Confederacy, he stayed in Washington as a Senator because he disagreed with the Southern secession. Lincoln asked Johnson to run with him for Vice President on the National Union ticket. Johnson became President when Lincoln died, just as the Civil War was ending.

Mrs. Lincoln refused to leave the White House, and Johnson's family was not able to move into the White House for several weeks after the inauguration. Mrs. Lincoln was allowed to remain in the White House to recover her health and get ready to move. During those last weeks, she let the White House steward go and so there was no one to oversee what went on. Crowds of people walked through the house, and many rooms were looted of valuable furnishings and ornaments. Even some of the beautiful curtains became torn and ragged as people took pieces for souvenirs. Mrs. Lincoln moved after five weeks had passed. The Johnsons were able to take up residence in the White House and begin to repair the destruction of the last weeks.

President Johnson's wife, Eliza, moved into the house with their two sons, two daughters, a son-in-law, and five grandchildren. Eliza had health problems, causing her to be unable to handle the daily schedule of being the hostess of the White House. Martha Patterson, her oldest daughter, agreed to take over the duties of hostess when her mother was not able. Mrs. Johnson was rarely able to attend any functions at the White House.

*First Lady Eliza Johnson, wife of President Andrew Johnson.*

The President's daughter Martha was well acquainted with Washington social etiquette. Her father had represented Tennessee in the Senate, 1857–1862. He was a Tennessee Democrat who did not join the Confederacy. He moved to Washington and did not give up his role in the Senate. In 1862, President Lincoln appointed him Military Governor of Tennessee. In 1864, Johnson was nominated to run as Vice President with Abraham Lincoln. Their ticket was elected.

Martha's husband, David T. Patterson, followed his father-in-law as a Senator from Tennessee. Martha had lived in Washington for quite a while and was well prepared to handle being hostess of the White House. Faced with the damage to the White House rooms, Martha began the long process of restoring them. Congress gave her money to refurbish the house, but it was much less than needed. She managed the money well and eventually was able to bring the White House back to its former glory.

## Morton in the Senate

President Johnson had been in office for about two years when Morton was elected to the Senate, and he quickly became the leader of the Republicans. In spite of the paralysis in his legs, his mind was sharp, and he was a strong and influential voice in Senate debates. He had a reputation of being a forceful and persuasive speaker. When the Senate was not in session, he kept a busy schedule of travel and speeches. When Morton came home from his first session in the Senate in the spring of 1867, he established a law partnership with E. B. Martindale and John S. Tarkington. Morton had invested wisely, especially in railroads, and had a reasonable income.

Expenses were high in Washington. Morton boarded in a hotel and employed secretaries and others to help him. Later, in December of 1870, Morton wrote that he could not afford the $450 a month at the National Hotel that he was paying and would have to look for cheaper lodgings. He also had three sons in private schools and both he and Lucinda traveled quite a bit. His sister-in-law and Lucinda's youngest sister, Sarah Gill, had lost her husband in 1867, after only two years of marriage. The Mortons provided a home and financial help for the young widow and her little daughter. Morton was the senior partner in the new law firm and the income from it would help with the extravagant expenses of living in Washington.

When Lucinda was in Washington, she attended social events with her husband. At times, he did not feel well and she attended alone. When she was not in residence, Morton tried to attend as many dinners and receptions as he could. December 1867, and January 1868, were the first holidays that he had been in the Senate. Lucinda was able to be with him in Washington. It was the custom to have lavish receptions on New Year's Day, given by the President and his Cabinet members. There were also many New Year's receptions given by other social leaders and politicians. Morton and other members of the Legislature were expected to visit the reception at the White House and those of the Cabinet members. It was optional for wives to attend with their husbands and they were free to host their own receptions.

The annual New Year's Day parties and receptions were elegant and very popular in Washington. It was reported in the Washington *Evening Star, 1868,* that Mrs. Senator Morton, along with several friends, "received the congratulations of many friends." They were all residents of the National Hotel where the reception was jointly held on January 1, 1868.

## President Johnson's Impeachment

Tensions were high on the political and social scene in Washington in early 1868. Reconstruction, or what to do with the defeated South, was an on-going and difficult situation for the President and Congress. In February, the U.S. House of Representatives passed a resolution to impeach President Andrew Johnson for "high crimes and misdemeanors," because of his handling of the Reconstruction

*A portrait of President Andrew Johnson taken by Matthew Brady.*

process. He was advocating President Lincoln's more lenient policy toward the Southern states. Johnson issued proclamations of general amnesty for those who would take an oath to support the Constitution. He reinstated former Confederates, both military and government officials. This enraged the Radical Republicans and others who demanded a harsher approach. It was the top issue between Congress and the President and they could not agree.

President Johnson removed Edwin Stanton, Secretary of War, from his Cabinet. Johnson was charged with breaching the Tenure of Office Act of 1867, which stated that the President could not dismiss appointed officials without the consent of Congress, a move that caused many legislators to turn against him. Eleven articles of impeachment were adopted by the House on March 2 and 3, 1868. The articles of impeachment were forwarded to the Senate.

The impeachment trial before the Senate was of great interest and controversy. The gallery seats were so much in demand that there were 1,000 color-coded tickets issued each day for seating. Each Senator received four tickets for observers. On March 22, 1868, according to the Washington *Evening Star*, "Nearly all the ladies known in fashionable circles in Washington accepted seats in the gallery, including Mrs. Morton." The floor of the chamber and the galleries were filled. The observers were glued to their seats as the trial moved forward. It was of national interest, and also a rich topic for gossip among the people of Washington.

*Illustration of the Senate's ladies' gallery during President Johnson's impeachment trial.*

When the final vote was taken in the Senate, late May 1868, thirty-five Senators voted for impeachment and nineteen against. Morton voted to impeach. Thirty-six votes were needed to impeach, making the vote one short of the majority and President Johnson was acquitted.

The tension between the Congress and President Johnson made the Washington social life hard for Lucinda and other women of the Republican Party. They had to attend social engagements and try to pretend that nothing had happened. The White House hostess, Mrs. Patterson, was credited with gracious behavior and calmness during this difficult time as her father completed the last few months of his term.

# Chapter 20

# LUCINDA AND JULIA GRANT

Ulysses S. Grant, the Republican candidate for President, was elected in 1868. He served from 1869–1877. His first Vice President was Schuyler Colfax, from Indiana. This was an ideal situation for Morton and Lucinda, for they were close friends with both men. Morton had supported Grant's campaign and given speeches for him. Grant's election helped overcome some of the bitterness and strife that the impeachment of Johnson had caused the Republicans. As usual with any President, the Grant administration had its own problems, successes, and scandals.

Grant's inauguration was on March 4, 1869, and the inaugural ball was held on March 20, in the north wing of the Treasury Department. It barely held the large crowd and there was no provision for heating. The ladies spent the evening wearing their wraps over their beautiful dresses and the men kept their coats and hats on.

Mrs. Julia Grant held her first reception in the White House on April 6, 1869. It was described as a grand affair. A large number of elegantly attired ladies and many gentlemen attended. All of Washington society was invited. Mrs. Grant, with three special friends, welcomed her guests to the Red Room in the White House. On her right was Mrs. Senator Morgan and on her left were Mrs. Senator Morton and Mrs. Senator Williams. After the initial greeting, the guests strolled through the Blue, Green, and East rooms that had been opened for them. The practice of opening several rooms in one's house for a reception or ball was a recent innovation. This allowed large numbers of guests to stroll freely through a larger area to greet each other without being crowded.

The description of the ladies' attire was an important detail to show the elegance of the affair. The *National Republican* newspaper of Washington, D.C., gave a description of the ladies. "Mrs. Grant wore a rich lavender colored silk, plainly trimmed with white lace, and without ornament. Her hair was slightly crimped in front with three curls dropping from her back hair.... Mrs. Morton wore a handsome purple silk without ornament, one curl on either side falling gracefully over a splendid white lace shawl."

Julia Grant was a strong-minded woman and the wife of a strong man. She had often visited her husband at his military postings during

*First Lady Julia Dent Grant, wife of President Ulysses S. Grant.*

the Civil War. Letters between them show she was a trusted confidante and he relied on her strength and encouragement. After General Robert E. Lee surrendered to Grant on April 9, 1865, the Grants came to Washington. The night of April 14, they were invited to attend the play at Ford's Theater with President and Mrs. Lincoln. They declined the invitation and narrowly escaped injury or death, for that was the night of Lincoln's assassination by John Wilkes Booth.

Mrs. Grant was an active first lady and enjoyed giving receptions, dinners, and parties in the White House. She kept up with what her husband was doing by attending Senate hearings. She was well acquainted with Cabinet members and others on the Washington political scene. Lucinda Morton was one of her close friends. She often helped Mrs. Grant with social affairs at the White House.

Morton stayed in Washington most of the time during the sessions of the Senate, although at times he made trips to give speeches or to visit home. There were always a number of important issues facing Congress that kept him busy. In his first term, Morton dealt with the issues of Reconstruction as the President and Congress worked to bring the defeated South back into the Union.

After serving some time in the Senate, Morton found himself viewing the plight of freed slaves in a different way than he had before the war ended. The matter of gaining civil rights for Black voters became important to him. He was a strong advocate for full citizenship for Blacks, including the right to vote. His strong backing for the Fifteenth Amendment to the Constitution helped pass it and Morton became a trusted friend of Black citizens. The amendment was ratified by the States in February 1870. He argued for the Enforcement Act of 1870–1871, sometimes called the Ku Klux Klan Act. It gave the President the power to oppose terrorism against Blacks in the South. Whatever issue was at the forefront of Morton's agenda, he thoroughly prepared his debate and was always ready to defend his position.

According to *The Olivia Letters,* an account of forty years worth of letters by a Washington correspondent, "His (Morton's) arguments are hurled at his opponent as cannonballs fly to kill the enemy." The writer also speaks of Senator Morton as the "highly gifted product of the great state of Indiana and in one sense the most interesting member of the United States Senate."

The Congress of 1869 began its session still contending with problems of the Reconstruction. There were always a number of important issues to consider and debate, and Morton had his hands full. Pain and poor health were always with him as he often described in his letters to Lucinda. He wrote to Lucinda almost every day when he was away, and she wrote back just as often. He told of his daily routine and described to her the events in the Senate. No doubt, Lucinda was concerned for him whenever they were apart.

President Grant counted on Morton as one of his best floor leaders in the Senate. He was such a valuable and persuasive politician that Grant offered him the position of minister to Great Britain. Morton considered the offer and felt that he would do well to accept it. However, in a letter to Lucinda, he wrote, "I said to the President that I will reserve the decision of the English matter until I return. I told him that you and I were both invalids, and that we could not live in the diplomatic style of Johnson and Motley, but he (Grant) said that poor health would be a good excuse for seeing as much or as little of company as we pleased."

Morton never took an important step in his career without considering Lucinda's opinion. Although it was prematurely reported that he had accepted the appointment to England, Morton ultimately decided not to become the minister to England and to keep his seat in the U.S. Senate.

It was also suggested to Morton that he be nominated to the Supreme Court. Lucinda was in favor of this, but others of his colleagues did not think it advisable because of his uncertain health. Morton preferred to be active in politics and not be stuck listening to court arguments.

There were many times during the Senate sessions when Morton was ill and sometimes he had to miss a Legislative session. He pushed himself to attend debates and votes. At times, he was barely able to speak and was so unsteady when walking with his crutches that he sometimes fell. Both his falls and other weaknesses were reported in the newspapers, but they also noted when he seemed to be doing better. No matter what he did or did not do, Morton continued to have both his supporters and his relentless critics in the press.

## A Prince in Washington

The year 1870 began with an exciting event for the society in Washington City. One of the most magnificent affairs of the season was the dinner and a Grand Ball given in honor of the visit of England's Prince Arthur to Washington. Nineteen-year-old Arthur William Patrick Albert was the seventh child and third son of Queen Victoria of the United Kingdom and her deceased husband, Prince Albert. Young Prince Arthur had recently completed military training and was commissioned a Lieutenant in the British Army.

Prince Arthur had made his first trip to visit the British province of Canada. He traveled south to visit the United States and especially the Capital City. The Prince stopped in New York where high society welcomed him with elaborate receptions and balls. He moved on to Washington and stayed with the British Minister to the U.S., Sir Edward Thornton. A short time after he arrived, a formal reception for him was given at the White House by President and Mrs. Grant.

The President's reception was an elaborate affair, with many guests. The rooms were richly decorated with patriotic symbols and flags under brilliant gaslights. Prince Albert's mother's picture (Queen Victoria) was hung so that it faced him as he dined. One reporter quipped that he did not know why Arthur would want to look at his mother while he was eating. Queen Victoria, after her husband's death in 1861, wore only black mourning clothing and a dour and unsmiling expression on her face in her portraits.

On January 27, 1870, the next grand event for Prince Arthur was a dinner given by Secretary of State Hamilton Fish and his wife. The many guests were seated for dinner at half-past six o'clock. After dinner, the guests retired to the library to enjoy their conversations. About nine o'clock, the guests proceeded to the Grand Ball given by the British Minister at the new Masonic Hall. It was said that seven hundred invitations had been sent, and according to reports, no one turned down the invitation.

No expense was spared by the British Minister to impress the Prince and the guests. The new hall was 140 feet deep and 40 feet wide. A raised platform for the Prince and his party was carpeted and arranged with sofas and comfortable armchairs. On the main floor, cane-seat chairs were arranged to seat two hundred people.

*Prince Arthur, Duke of Connaught and Strathearn, son of Queen Victoria and Prince Albert.*

The freshly waxed floors gleamed, ready for dancing. Flags of all nations were hung in unique designs around the hall, with British and American flags most prominent. Fresh flower wreaths were hung on the side gaslights. The elaborate lighting was described by the Washington *Evening Star*:

> *The hall was lighted with eighteen three-pronged side-brackets, in enamel and gilt, and on each prong a 'crown' shed forth light from three burners. In front of the music gallery was an elaborate lighting design with the center piece being a six-point star formed of gas jets, and on either side of the star shown ten brilliant gaslights.*

The Prince arrived at a quarter to ten, dressed in his splendid uniform with the Order of the Garter, studded with jewels, on his chest. All the dignitaries attending the ball wore their most splendid uniforms or dress clothing. The women wore their most beautiful and elegant gowns and hair arrangements. The newspaper declared that, "this was one of the most brilliant and enjoyable affairs which had ever enlivened Washington society."

A few of the ladies were singled out and their dresses described. Early on the list was Mrs. Senator Morton. She wore "a pearl-colored moiré antique (sometimes called watered silk) with rich lace trimming, and a black lace Basque (jacket) and overskirt; with diamond ornaments." Mrs. Morton was an attractive lady at age forty-five, and was often noted for her attire when attending social events in Washington. After a midnight supper, the ball continued until at least three o'clock when the Prince left.

With money always in short supply for the Mortons, one may wonder how Lucinda was able to come up with elaborate and elegant gowns for so many events. Women of society tried to appear to have new gowns for important social events. The elaborate gowns were usually made by dressmakers and exclusively for each client. With each skirt, at least two tops were made so that outfits could appear different. It was acceptable for an elegant gown to be worn more than one time if the jewels and other adornments were changed. The beautiful gowns could not be set aside because they were so expensive.

*An illustration showing a gown with changeable tops.*

Women of the Victorian times were clever at finding ways to make their outfit look fresh and different. One could change the collar, wear different jewelry, change the hairstyle, add a new hat or shawl, and change the trimmings on the dress. Lucinda was known to be an expert seamstress and would know how to make changes to her dresses.

Styles for women's skirts had changed from large hoops in the 1860s to a flatter front and a bustle. The bustle of the 1870s had a softer, more drape-like back. By the 1880s, the bustle on women's skirts became like a high shelf behind the waist, causing manufacturers to make special chairs so the women in high-fashion dresses could sit down comfortably. Because of the large amount of material in the hooped skirts of the 1860s, Lucinda could have had some of her elegant 1860s gowns redesigned for the new fashion.

## Lucinda is Injured From a Fall

A little later in 1870, after the exciting January events, Lucinda and Morton visited their family in Centerville. The living quarters of Lucinda's parents were on the second story of Isaac Burbank's store building. While visiting her parents, Lucinda was carrying her sister's young daughter down the steep back stairs when she turned, made a misstep, and fell. As she turned, she put the little girl down, but continued to fall to the bottom. Lucinda's head was thrown back almost under her shoulder. It stayed that way for several hours. Finally, it was determined that her neck was not broken, and it was gently moved back into place. Morton did not return to Washington until she was pronounced out of danger. The fall left her with recurring problems and pain in her neck and face.

According to the March 8, 1870 *Evansville Journal,* "Mrs. Senator Morton is still confined to her bed, at the residence of her parents at Centreville (old spelling), from the effects of injuries received two weeks ago, by falling down a pair of stairs. She is mending gradually." Lucinda was well enough to return to Washington in May. Whenever Lucinda was in Washington, she was a frequent guest to receptions and events. When the Senate was not in session, Lucinda returned to her Indianapolis home.

During the year 1870, Morton's father, James Throck Morton, passed away at the home of his daughter, Anna Marie Hart, in Keokuk, Iowa. He had been ill with the same type of affliction that paralyzed his son.

## Back Home Again

Governor Baker moved out of the Morton house by the fall of 1870, as soon as he found another place for his family. The Morton house in Indianapolis was located on the southeast corner of Pennsylvania Street and New York Street, facing the First Presbyterian Church and close to the Baptist Church. Several other churches were close by. Lucinda was a member of the Central Christian Church, earlier known as the Christian Chapel, at the corner of Delaware Street and Ohio Street.

Morton's son, John Morton, completed his education at the North West Christian University, a prestigious school in Indianapolis. The Disciples of Christ, the denomination of the Central Christian Church, had approved the University's charter in 1850 and it opened its doors in 1856. Ovid Butler was the most prominent among those who raised the needed funds. The name of the University was changed to Butler University after John Morton had graduated. The school moved from its original site to Irvington in 1877. A larger campus was needed and a campus was formed in 1928 on the site of Fairview Park, a former amusement park on the Indianapolis' northwest side. The University was the second in Indiana and the third in the nation to admit men, women, and people of color.

Ovid Butler was the President of the school's Board of Directors until 1871. Demia Butler, his daughter, was the first woman to graduate from the Classical course at the university. She passed away in 1867. To honor her memory, Mr. Butler endowed the Demia Butler Chair of English Literature and the position was designated for a woman professor. Catharine Merrill was the first to occupy the chair and the second female university professor in the country.

When the Mortons were at home in Indianapolis, they had many visitors. While giving an interview to a reporter at their home in 1871, the Presbyterian bells began to ring. The lady reporter from the *Indianapolis Sun* wrote:

> *"There's that bell again!" observed Mrs. Morton.*
>
> *"Did you ever hear the like?' he (Morton) replied, turning to me. "They have a new sexton and he doesn't know how to ring the bell. He keeps it thundering at that rate for an hour. We are driven off our own doorstep by it."*

Although the house was located across the street from several magnificent residences, the Senator's house was of the plainest description. It was a double house, two-and-a-half stories high, and had a tasteful iron veranda across the front, which opened into both entrances. The house had been made into a one-family residence. Morton's favorite place was the back parlor that looked out on the Baptist Church.

*The Morton's home in Indianapolis.*

A large double parlor was on one side with a small library just beyond. The back parlor connected to the dining room with folding doors that could be opened to host large social engagements. The furnishings of the house were described as rich, but plain. In the front parlor were hung fine paintings, including portraits of President Lincoln, General Sherman, and President Grant. The living room and parlor were adorned with photographs of their family. A large comfortable lounge sat beside the grate where the Senator could be found most of the day. The moment any visitor enters the parlor, he rises to a sitting position, and "with hand, voice and eye, extends a cordial welcome." Their callers were friends, political acquaintances, reporters, and family members. Lucinda had become used to a busy and interrupted home life when she was in charge of the Governor's House.

Their house had cost $12,000, but the Mortons were not rich people. According to this same newspaper article, "Of carriages, he has one, a much-worn two-seated vehicle, which is drawn by an old black horse much the worse for spavin (*old and decrepit*)." His carriage driver complained that the carriage and nag are the "sore distress and daily mortification" of him. Morton also used this carriage in Washington.

The lady reporter titled one section of the article*, Senator Morton and the Ladies.* She wrote that he was fond of lady visitors and especially if they could sing. He loved to attend concerts and the opera when he had time and could hum or sing many melodies that he heard performed.

Morton was fond of his home, but seldom enjoyed it. He spent a lot of time traveling to make speeches or trying to find relief for his disability and pain. He did not like to have his movements advertised. Lucinda agreed with him and supported him in his travels to seek treatment.

Lucinda is described in the same 1871 article as being "possessed of uncommon ability, is a shrewd observer, and there is nothing in politics that she does not know. But she is modest to a charm and hasn't a particle of nonsense about her. In person she is below the medium height, slightly built, and has a graceful bearing. She has a well-shaped head and comely features. Her smile is lovely, and her eyes and voice bewitching. She is fine, the most womanly of women. Perhaps because he has found his wife so sterling and capable [makes him better] as Senator."

## Scandals and Blackmail

When they were apart, Morton kept in close touch with letters. He addressed his letters to "My Dear Wife' and signed them "Yours In Love." He signed some letters with "Love to the children and to you." His letters often closed with loving regards to his wife, such as "… Love to you as ever devoted in life to death." His signatures, even to family, were the formal *O. P. Morton*.

During the Victorian era, it was the common practice to address your spouse as Mr. or Mrs. when in the company of others. Calvin Fletcher, who wrote his diaries in Indiana from 1817 to 1866, always referred to his wife as Mrs. Fletcher, but used the first names of other women in his writings.

Morton suffered a lot of pain as he expressed in his letter of December 12, 1870.

"My dear wife, I went to the Senate today with great labor, was carried by stout Negroes in a chair from the carriage to the door of the chamber and back in the same way." He continued,

"I have been worried by Mrs. Jim Pritchet. She has been here three times and yesterday I gave orders to the boy at the front door to always say I was out. She was drunk every time she came, and told the boy that she was my daughter-in-law, that she was the wife of Johnny Morton. Today she came to the Senate and sent in for me, but I refused to go out. She then sent in a note wanting to borrow $15.00. I sent her word I could not let her have it. She wrote back that she must have it and that she would wait until I came out. What to do I did not know, but was afraid of a scene and sent her $10.00."

"When she was here yesterday she said a copy of that Philadelphia paper containing that vile article had been sent to Dr. Pritchet, and intimated that Mary Pritchet had sent it to her friends in Indianapolis. She did not say this right out but gave me to understand it. She said that Lida had seen it and cried. She is desperate and sickly and I don't know how to get clear of her." The Lida referred to by Mrs. Prichett (the correct spelling of the last name) was Mrs. William Holloway, Lucinda's sister Eliza, who lived in Indianapolis.

Lucinda and Morton would have known about Mrs. James Prichett because they had lived in Centerville and their families still lived there. They would have heard the local gossip about her and they were acquainted with her husband, James.

Dr. John Prichett was a Centerville doctor with a fine reputation who had served in the Civil War. His son, James graduated from the U.S. Naval Academy in 1857. He was assigned to the Washington Navy Yard in 1861. He met and married Alice Lee that December. When the Civil War started, James joined the Naval forces on the Mississippi in 1862. In 1863, he won praise for the winning action against a superior Confederate force during the Battle of Helena, Arkansas. He became the Commander of the monitor *USS Mahopac* during the war. After the war, James sailed with Admiral Farragut to Russia and in 1869, returned to the Pacific Squadron. Lieutenant Commander Prichett was serving with the *USS Vermont* at the Brooklyn Navy Yard, when he became ill and died in 1874. He was buried in Crown Hill Cemetery in Centerville, Indiana.

Alice Lee Prichett was originally from Washington City. While her husband, James, was serving with the Navy, she gave birth to three children, one son and two daughters. She lived in Centerville with James' family. It is not clear how many of their children survived. The continued absence of her husband and living in a tiny town so different from Washington, could have caused her depression, drinking, and foolish behavior. She would have been dependent upon her father-in-law for support, since military benefits were not enough to support a family.

At the time Alice was living in Centerville, the town was "dry" and only certain grocery stores were allowed to sell liquor for medicinal purposes. But for those who were determined to have it, drinking liquor could be found. Alice's drunkenness would have been choice gossip for the town. Her behavior would have been a disgrace for the doctor's family. This was sad for everyone, as James Prichett was one of Centerville's most distinguished young men.

*Lieutenant Commander James M. Prichett.*

The story of James Prichett does not end at his death. During WW II in 1942, the Navy was searching for a name for the new ship to be ready for service. They searched former names of Naval heroes and came across James Prichett's distinguished service record. A ship was named the *USS Prichett* in his honor. It was commissioned in January 1944. The ship saw battle in the Pacific Ocean, the China Sea, Iwo Jima, and Okinawa, during WW II. In 1946, it was decommissioned and berthed with the San Diego Pacific Reserve Fleet. In 1952, the ship was sent out to serve in the Korean Conflict. From 1955–1970, the *USS Prichett* was sent on various tours, as well as to Vietnam. The ship returned to San Diego and was decommissioned and struck from the Navy List in January 1970. The ship was sold to Italy and renamed the *Geniere.* She was stricken and scrapped in 1975.

It is doubtful that Lucinda gave much attention to Alice Prichett's charges, knowing her reputation, and she trusted Morton. But it was disturbing to realize how much trouble her demands and accusations were causing Morton in Washington. His enemies had made up many vicious stories about Morton having affairs and womanizing. The stories resurfaced every so often and were printed again by politically rival newspapers to try to harm his reputation.

## The District of Columbia

In February 1871, Morton wrote in detail to Lucinda, describing the celebration for the new consolidation of the District of Columbia. The major political subdivisions were incorporated into one, and the Organic Act of 1871 provided for a new reconstructed local government for the District of Columbia.

Morton described the celebration of the event for Lucinda, "The crowd upon the Avenue yesterday was estimated at from 75,000 to 100,000. The performances were very poor and even contemptible. But the illumination last night was beautiful beyond anything I had ever seen. Nearly every house from the Capitol to the Treasury Department was lighted and thousands of Chinese lanterns suspended on ropes, and calcium light as bright almost as the sun, made the street brilliant as noon day."

Morton could not always attend events, but could observe them from hotel windows. He had first lived in the National Hotel in Washington, but was able to move to the Ebbitt House Hotel. After he moved, he wrote to son Walter that their rooms were only ten

*Ebbitt House Hotel.*

feet from the elevator. The elevator was thirty feet to the pavement and "… we are better fixed than we have ever been in Washington."

In a letter on April 4, 1871, Morton had written of his concern for his 15-year-old son, Walter. "I am greatly troubled about Walter. This leaving school and going off visiting where he is under no restraint will have a bad effect upon him I fear. Would it not be better to require him to go to school unless he is sick and in that case keep him at home? If he is not dealt with firmly now in a year or two I fear his case will be hopeless."

Like many young adventurers, ultimately, Walter did not disappoint his parents. He was to prove intelligent and a son to be proud of. Morton could not see it, but Walter was following his father's restless spirit and a love for travel and adventure.

The life of a Senator in Washington was always full of political business as well as the social duties. Lucinda knew what was going on with Morton from his letters, as he wrote about the political scene and how he was feeling. In the same letter of April 4 concerning Walter, Morton tells of giving a speech in the Senate when several disgruntled Republican Senators went into a cloakroom while he was speaking. He ignored them, but when he finished his speech, he was so weak he could "scarce sit in my chair." He says that the warm weather in Washington had made him feel weak.

Despite his affliction and pain, Morton continued to be invited to make speeches around the country. His reputation as a statesman and his unrelenting stand for what he believed in made him a popular speaker and a strong Senator. He had taken up the cause of civil rights for the Black American men and suffrage for women. There were those who opposed both issues in his own party, but he was relentless in championing these causes.

In early 1871, Grant signed into law the first Civil Rights Act that gave the President the power to suspend the writ of habeas corpus and to use federal forces to combat the Ku Klux Klan. Other political groups were attacking the civil rights of the newly freed Black Americans and this law also applied to them. The Act bolstered the enforcement of the Fourteenth Amendment and the Civil Rights Act of 1866.

The year 1872 was filled with the planning for the next Presidential election as Grant was up for reelection. All year there were conventions to attend, speeches to give, and the business of the Senate. Grant and Morton were close friends and they worked together to help elect Republican candidates. Morton attended as many state and county Republican conventions and rallies as he was able, giving speeches and reminding his listeners that it was the Democrat Party that supported the rebellion and was responsible for the violence in the

*President Ulysses S. Grant served from 1869–1877.*

South. The many invitations to speak were an honor and added to his national reputation. His frequent appearances and persuasive speeches strengthened his leadership of the Republican Party. The Democrats were just as determined to challenge their opponents. Their speeches were against the Republican control, the handling of civil rights issues, and the way the Reconstruction of the South was handled.

In November, President Grant was reelected and the Republicans gained sixty more seats in Congress. Morton's term as Indiana Senator was up in January 1873. The Indiana Senate overwhelmingly reelected him in late November 1872, instead of waiting for his term to expire. The early vote was a show of support for him in Indiana.

Even though Morton traveled and gave many speeches, he was always trying to find help for his pain and paralysis. Periodically, he took the "waters" at Hot Springs, Arkansas. It seemed to help the pain and give him much-needed rest.

Morton was encouraged about son Walter. In early December 1872, his letter to Walter says, "We were very glad to get your letter and read it over again. We are so glad you are happy, and hope and have no doubt you are doing well at school." Walter had repented of his careless attitude toward his studies and began to take his education seriously, attending school, and working hard to achieve good grades.

He concludes his letter by reminding Walter that he is sending three dollars "for Ollie Scott's skates, and shall not forget the diamond earrings. Give our love to Aunt Lida, Uncle Will, and Eddie. God bless you and keep you. O. P. Morton"

The people mentioned in this letter are Oliver Morton Scott (Ollie Scott), the son of Lucinda's sister, Rachel Scott. The skates for this gift may have been roller skates, as this was becoming a popular sport. Aunt Lida and Uncle Will were Eliza, Lucinda's sister, and her husband, William Holloway. Their only son, Eddie, was a little younger than Lucinda's son, Oliver T. Brother-in-law Holloway often took care of business for Morton in Indianapolis when he or Lucinda had to be away. He was especially kind and helpful at the time of Morton's last illness and death.

In January 1873, Morton wrote from Washington to Holloway. "Lucinda's condition is very sad and distressing. Her suffering is intense except when under the influence of morphia (morphine) and she gets sleep in no other way. She has been confined to her bed for eight days and is deeply discouraged and so am I, for she cannot stand this suffering a great while."

After the 1873 spring session of the Senate ended, Lucinda must have recovered somewhat from her illness so they could make a trip to Idaho Springs in Colorado. Idaho Springs was a young town, having been the place of the Colorado Gold Rush in 1859. The warm springs on Soda Creek had been used by the Arapahoe Native Americans and they considered springs to be sacred. In 1863, Dr. E. M. Cummings invested in the property and set up the first public health baths. Since those times, people from all over the world have come to the Hot Springs of Colorado to enjoy the effects of the baths. The hot springs can still be visited today.

*An aerial view of Idaho Springs, Colorado.*

While they were in Colorado, Morton wrote again to his brother-in-law, Will Holloway. He reported that Lucinda still was not well and that they both were discouraged. She suffered from neuralgia, especially at night when she tried to sleep and she was losing strength. The type of neuralgia that Lucinda experienced was probably caused by the fall she had on the stairs of her parents' home. It is called Trigeminal neuralgia and is associated with pain from the Trigeminal nerve that travels from the brain and branches to different parts of the face. It can be caused by a blood vessel pressing down on the nerve where it meets with the brainstem. No doubt, there was considerable trauma to Lucinda's head when she fell and received such a hard blow.

The letter also contained the request that Holloway ask Mrs. McKenna if she would board Lucinda while the house was being fixed. Gas lighting and a coal furnace were being installed in their home in Indianapolis. Gas was becoming available in homes for lighting. When Lucinda was not able to be at home in Indianapolis, she preferred to stay with Mrs. McKenna. Holloway was watching over the installations at the house.

After the trip to Colorado, Morton felt better. His hot springs treatments helped him to walk and stand easier. In November, he wrote to Lucinda that he was concerned that she had not improved as he had hoped. He was still feeling better and was able to walk with only one cane, but sometimes still used his crutches.

# Chapter 21

# WEDDINGS AND MORE IN 1874

The Morton boys were able to visit their parents on holidays and at other times when they were in residence in Washington. Their oldest son, John, came to visit them and his fiancé. He was engaged to Harriet Brown, the daughter of S. P. Brown of Washington, D.C.

John Morton and Harriet (Hattie) Brown were married on February 13, 1874 at Mount Pleasant, home of the bride. Only the two families and a few friends attended. Among the guests were President Grant and his son, Lieutenant Fred Grant; Speaker James Blaine; and Senators Hannibal Hamlin and Lot M. Morrill, of Maine. Although the wedding was private, it was described as lavish and beautiful. All the ladies were handsomely dressed and the mother of the groom, Mrs. Morton, was among the most noticeable.

The wedding report added, "A pleasing feature of this charming reunion was the number of blooming children straying among the guests, and by their bright presence dispelling formality and suggesting future happy occasions of a similar nature."

John and Hattie left on the train for a trip to Boston, New York, and Niagara Falls. They returned to Washington, and after a few weeks, traveled to their home in San Francisco, California. John would be working with the Alaskan Commercial Company. This company had a monopoly for taking fur seals on the Aleutian Islands. Later, John was appointed an agent with the Treasury Department to oversee that no more than the one hundred thousand seals per year were taken. John's appointment to a position in the Treasury Department received criticism for this political post. It was felt that since he had worked for the Alaskan company for several years and had a financial interest in it, that he would be inclined to give favor to the company. However, it was shown that neither John nor Senator Morton owned any stock in the company.

The Mortons were invited to the wedding of Nellie Grant, the only daughter of President and Mrs. Grant. It took place on May 21, 1874, and was the most important event of the Washington social season. Nellie was not quite nineteen when she married Algernon Sartoris. She had met her future husband on board the ship as she was returning from a trip to Europe in 1872. He was the second son of a member of the British Parliament and was heir to the family estate. His older brother had died, and would have inherited the title and estate, being the oldest son. But his sad death left Algernon as the oldest living son. He expected to have an income of $40,000 a year.

President and Mrs. Grant were concerned about the match and insisted that the couple could not marry for at least a year. They were not favorably impressed with Sartoris because he was a "drinking man." But because their daughter was so determined, they finally agreed to the marriage. A few years later, the couple divorced, because as one person described him, "he was a drunken fool," who had abused his wife and family.

Ellen Wrenshall Grant was born on July 4, 1855. She had lived quietly with her parents and was not accustomed to high society. She was thrust into the exciting world of Washington at age fourteen in 1869, when her father was elected President. In 1872, to keep Nellie out of the spotlight, Grant sent her on a trip to Europe. In England, she was received by Queen Victoria and attended many garden parties.

The Queen described Nellie as "rather stiff and off hand in her manner and spoke with a great twang."

Since 1820, there had been three weddings in the White House. The first was President Monroe's daughter, Maria, to Samuel L. Gouverneur. The second was Lizzie Tyler, daughter of President John Tyler, wed to William Waller in 1843. Nellie Grant's wedding was the third, in 1874. Her dress was extravagant and said to be worth thousands. The marriage was conducted in the East Room of the White House that was lavishly decorated with flowers. It was estimated that there were less than 200 guests and family, and it was considered to be private. Among the guests were Senator and Mrs. Morton. The gifts were displayed in the library, and it was estimated that their value was at least $60,000. President Grant gave them a check for $10,000.

*The wedding of Nellie Grant and Algernon Sartoris.*

Morton made many speeches for President Grant and the Republicans during the summers after the Senate sessions were over. In 1874, he spoke of his concern about schools for Black children. He agreed that if there were enough Black students, they could have their own schools. But if there were only a few Black children in a community, they should be allowed to attend the white schools. This, of course, had many dissenting politicians up in arms and both sides were, as usual, bitterly opposing each other.

During that summer, Morton became so ill that he had taken to his bed for a week or so. In September, he took a trip to California with Lucinda, her sister Eliza Holloway, Mrs. William H. English, and her daughter. Morton spent several weeks at the Hot Springs of Santa Barbara in another attempt to regain his health. The soaking in the hot spring probably helped both him and Lucinda in their particular disabilities. Morton felt much better when he returned to Washington in December 1874.

The next short Congressional session began in December and ended on March 24, 1875. In April, Morton and Lucinda, along with other Senators, their wives, and friends, were invited on a pleasure trip to Mexico. The invitation came from Senator Angus Cameron and Thomas A. Scott, President of the Pennsylvania R.R. When the party reached New Orleans, the reports of yellow fever in Vera Cruz and other places were confirmed. The trip was called off, so the party stayed for a few days in New Orleans. Morton and Lucinda were welcomed and entertained by Republican friends in the city. Morton felt well while he was there and was encouraged when he returned to Indianapolis.

## Morton for President

In 1875, several candidates began to emerge for the Republican nominee for President in the 1876 election. After much consideration, by late 1875, President Grant had decided not to seek a third term.

Since Morton was the leader in the Senate, he seemed a likely candidate for President. At first, it was just speculation that Morton would run, but rumors circulated that he would seek election on the Republican ticket. He did begin to campaign for the office in the summer of 1875.

Articles were being printed both *for* Morton's election and *against* it, citing his physical problems and other charges of unfitness. Indiana Governor Thomas Hendricks was seeking the nomination for President on the Democrat ticket. He was the party's eventual nominee for Vice President. During the campaign, Morton and Hendricks conducted a fierce campaign of speeches, not sparing anything against the other. The newspapers had lots of material to fuel their fires of controversy between the two parties.

At the 1876 Republican National Convention in Cincinnati, Morton's name was offered as a candidate. He was not able to gain enough votes, and the convention nominated Rutherford B. Hayes, Governor of Ohio, as the Republican candidate for President. He won the election and became the 19th President of the United States. Morton was a strong supporter of Hayes during the campaign and they became fast friends.

## Morton and Women's Suffrage

The serious effort for women's suffrage had begun in the 1850s. When the Civil War started, the cause of women's rights and temperance took a backseat to the need to help with the war effort. As soon as the Civil War was over, women began to hold meetings and conventions to persuade states and territories to give women the right to vote. The West was rapidly expanding, and in 1869, those supporting the effort for suffrage were able to convince the Territorial Legislature of Wyoming to pass a resolution allowing women to vote. The law also guaranteed that teachers, both male and female, should have equal pay. Another bill guaranteed that married women could have property rights separate from their husbands and that they should have the same legal rights. Although there was opposition, full suffrage for women was signed into law on December 10, 1869, and Wyoming was the first state government in the United States to guarantee women's suffrage.

Morton had seen firsthand the value of women's work during the Civil War. His own wife was an example of leadership as the Governor's wife and the leader of society. She planned and organized events and groups of ladies to help supply the soldiers' needs. It was Lucinda's careful and thoughtful management of these things that added so much help to his work and the success of his time as Governor. He understood the intelligence, perseverance, and creativity of women. He needed no persuasion to champion their rights.

In June 1871, Senator Morton had been asked to speak to the alumni of the State University in Bloomington, Indiana, the present Indiana University. The classes of the university were open to women as well as men, and the curriculum was the same for both. It seemed appropriate for him to consider the rights of women as part of his speech. This was the first public declaration of his support as a Senator for women's suffrage.

A bill was put forth in 1874 to the Territorial Legislature that the Dakota Territory be divided, with the new territory to be called Pembina. An amendment was offered to the bill that gave women the right to vote. This was fiercely debated, with strong arguments on both sides, and Morton speaking for the cause of equal rights for women.

Women in most states were not allowed to own property, and "common law" gave their fathers or husbands all legal rights to make decisions for them. Morton disagreed and spoke with logical arguments for women's rights. Unfortunately, for the cause of women's suffrage in the proposed Pembina, those opposing were able to defeat the amendment and stop the making of a new territory. It was not until 1889 that the Dakota Territory was split into North and South. Later

*Women's Rights Convention in Washington, D.C.*

that year, North Dakota and South Dakota were admitted to the Union as the 39th and 40th states.

The rights of women continued to be a widely debated topic across the country in the 1870s. It was debated in state legislatures, in Congress, and in newspapers and magazines. Because of his speeches in the 1874 debates, Morton was considered one of its strongest political supporters. Leaders of the movement gained strength and determination. He gave speeches at their conventions and he and Lucinda were friends with many influential leaders of the movement. Morton continued to advocate for equal rights for women throughout the rest of his life. Ever since he had been in the Senate, Morton had supported full political suffrage for Black citizens and for Native Americans. He clearly was in favor of equal rights for all citizens of the United States, without discrimination.

The year 1876 started with a busy schedule of social gatherings and political events. At the end of January, John Morton and his wife, Hattie, visited Lucinda and Morton in Washington. They stayed with her parents because the Mortons had only a few rooms at the Ebbitt House Hotel. Lucinda entertained friends one afternoon with the help of her daughter-in-law and Mrs. Colonel Hart. It was described in the newspaper as "being held in Mrs. Morton's very cozy parlor with a host of warm friends. Callers were received with charming hospitality." The report enthusiastically described Lucinda, "Mrs. Morton is one of the most amiable and entertaining ladies in Washington, and one of society's real ornaments."

On the evening of February 20, Lucinda attended "A Pleasant Hop at the Ebbitt House" given by Mr. Willard. It was a supper with music and dancing. Names that were listed were mostly women, but with such an event, men must have also attended. As usual, Washington society filled its days and nights with receptions, teas, concerts, theater, and formal dinners. Morton enjoyed musical evenings, and a few days before the "Pleasant Hop," he, Lucinda, John's wife, Hattie, and her parents attended the opera.

# Chapter 22

# A VERY SPECIAL MEMORIAL

On April 14, large crowds came to Washington, D.C. to commemorate the $11^{th}$ anniversary of President Abraham Lincoln's death. A joint resolution by Congress had declared it a legal holiday. A large 12-foot tall statue of Lincoln, standing on a 10-foot base, was to be unveiled on Lincoln Square. The square had been used as a hospital area for wounded troops during the Civil War. Congress officially named it Lincoln Square in 1869. This would be the first memorial of Lincoln to be placed in the Nation's Capital.

The statue of Lincoln was designed by Thomas Ball and paid for by contributions from freed slaves and Black regiments of soldiers who served in the Civil War. This money was given sacrificially by people who had very little.

The day after hearing of the assassination of President Lincoln in 1865, Charlotte Scott, a freed Black woman living in Ohio, spoke to her employer. She gave him five dollars, the first money she had earned after her freedom by the Emancipation Proclamation. She asked that it be used to start a fund to pay for a statue of President Lincoln. The money was sent to the Western Sanitary Commission and word spread to the Black community all over the nation. Funds were collected from 1865 to 1873, when the amount was large enough to contract with a sculptor.

When the statue fund was started, it was made clear that all the money must come from the freed slaves, Black military regiments, and other Black citizens. This was to be their tribute to the man who had set them free. To understand the value of money given by the Black Union soldiers, a private's pay during the Civil War was only $13 a month. The average given by each of the soldiers in the 70th U.S. Colored Infantry from Mississippi in 1865 was $4.32, about one-third of a month's pay for many.

Thomas Ball, an American artist, sculptor, and musician, was on his way home from Italy when he heard the news of Lincoln's death. He said, "I could not free myself from the horror of it during the rest of my journey." When he reached home, he designed his own memorial, a half-life size statue of Lincoln breaking the chains to set a slave free. It was from this original design that the final Emancipation Statue was made.

Ball was given the contract to design and make the statue in 1873. The amount raised was only $17,000, much less than a large bronze statue would ordinarily cost. But Ball was so touched by the circumstances of raising the funds that he accepted it for his fee. He stated, "Of course I accepted their offer, for you must remember that every cent of this money was contributed by freed men and women."

The statue was built in Italy and cast in bronze. It was carefully shipped to the U.S. and was allowed to pass through customs duty-free. Congress granted $3,000 for the base, and on its day of unveiling, the statue was covered in American flags. The general invitation to attend the ceremony was given out to "friends of impartial freedom, equal rights and free institutions our country over" to come and celebrate. They encouraged "colored fellow-citizens, who honor themselves especially in the erection of the monument, to send full delegations from all over the country."

The crowd was estimated at 25,000. President Grant introduced and unveiled the gleaming statue to cheering and applause. On the stage were the President, the Cabinet, Senate members and Representatives, and many other dignitaries. More enthusiastic applause greeted the famous former slave Frederick Douglass, who gave the dedication speech. It was a wonderful day of coming together for all races in Washington. From that time, the memorial in Lincoln Park of Lincoln setting the slave free has been known as the *Emancipation Memorial*.

*"Emancipation Memorial."*

Almost 100 years later in 1974, a second statue was added to Lincoln Park. Mary McLeod Bethune, the daughter of a slave, became one of the foremost Black educators and advocates for civil rights from the late 1890s to 1955. She served in a federal agency under four Presidents and is the first woman and the first African–American to be honored with a statue on public parkland in Washington, D.C. The Lincoln statue was turned so that the two faced each other in Lincoln Park.

*"Mary McLeod Bethune Memorial."*

Senator Morton was not mentioned in the press accounts of the celebration. But because he was very active in advocating for African-American civil rights and for them to be represented in Congress, he would have made it a priority to attend.

A few days after the celebration of the *Emancipation Memorial*, Lucinda received word that her father, Isaac Burbank, had been severely injured in a fall at his home on north Ninth Street in Richmond, Indiana. He was 88 and described as "old and feeble." He passed away a few days later, on April 23. His wife, Mary, and six of their children were together before his death. His oldest son, Edward, was in Germany, and was not able to get home.

Isaac Burbank and his wife had owned the mercantile business in Centerville until 1870, when they moved to Richmond to be closer to their children. Isaac's grave is in the Crown Hill Cemetery in Centerville. He and Mary were members of the Presbyterian Church in Centerville.

## The World's Fair in Philadelphia

More excitement was on the way for the nation when the Centennial Exposition, the first official World's Fair held in the United States, opened on May 10, 1876 in Philadelphia, Pennsylvania. Thirty-seven countries participated and the fair buildings covered many acres of the Fairmount Park. President Grant and Emperor Pedro II of Brazil opened the fair by starting the Corliss engines that had been built especially to power the exhibits at the Exposition. Joining the President and the Emperor on the podium were several candidates for the Presidency and other offices, including Morton. He also took part when the Exposition closed.

It is very likely that Lucinda and her two youngest sons were able to attend the Exposition at a later time. Both Walter and Oliver T. were still of school age. Walter attended the Pennsylvania Military

Academy in West Chester, Pennsylvania, where he was in his third year, studying civil engineering. Oliver T. was still a year from graduating from preparatory school. Their oldest son, John, lived in California at the time.

Among the interesting exhibits at the Exposition from the United States was the National Women's Suffrage Association. They prepared an exhibit in the Women's Pavilion to advertise and declare their "Declaration of Rights of Women." In other buildings, many new inventions were shown, such as the typewriter, mass-produced sewing machines, stoves, lanterns, wagons, carriages, and agricultural equipment. Alexander Graham Bell's telephone and Thomas Edison's automatic telegraph system were demonstrated to curious crowds. New delights for the taste buds were popcorn, root beer, and catsup. Everyone who could afford to attend did so. Since the fair lasted several months, many people returned several times to see the wonders of this massive fair with exhibits from all over the world. No doubt, the Morton family, and especially young Walter, marveled at all the new innovations and inventions.

# Chapter 23

# A NEW PRESIDENT

Although the Republican Convention did not nominate Morton for President in the summer of 1876, he immediately threw himself into a busy schedule of travel and speeches. He fully supported the Republican Presidential nominee, Rutherford B. Hayes. Morton and Hayes had campaigned together and become friends during the Civil War and when Hayes was running for Governor of Ohio. President Hayes was elected in November, and because he did not win the popular vote, but did win the electoral vote, the Democrats disputed the election. The hotly contested race could not be finally resolved until the Congressional session, which began in December 1876. After much controversy and negotiations between the parties, a compromise was reached and President Rutherford B. Hayes was sworn into office on March 5, 1877.

Morton never spared himself when it came to traveling for political speeches or his work in the Senate. He had to be carried into the Senate building and could walk only for short distances with his crutches or cane. He gave his speeches while sitting. Even though his body was weak, he seemed to be able to focus his whole strength into his strong, compelling speeches. Lucinda spent as much time as possible with him in Washington. After the busy Christmas holidays in the capital city, she returned to Indiana for a ten-day visit in January 1877.

Lucinda was attentive to Morton's frequent ill health. She traveled with him whenever possible. She is described in one article as standing by his side and gently rubbing his forehead as if he had a headache. As the Congressional session of 1877 unfolded, Morton continued to meet political obligations as much as possible, although he seemed to be having more incidents of weakness and ill health.

President Hayes took the oath of office on March 5, 1877, on the East Portico of the United States Capitol building. His wife, Lucy Hayes, was the third President's wife that Lucinda had worked with while Morton was in the Senate. The couples were friends, since the husbands had been colleagues for many years. There was no inaugural ball in 1877 because the election was still uncertain. The new Presidential term began on an uneasy footing.

*President Rutherford B Hayes.*

The first official state dinner was on April 10, to honor foreign diplomats. A "full quota of wine" was served to guests. Shortly after this, President Hayes made it known that no more alcoholic beverages would be served at White House functions. The Hayes family was known to be teetotalers (did not drink alcohol), although occasionally they had served mild alcoholic drinks to guests in their home in Ohio. Lucy was strongly in favor of temperance.

*First Lady Lucy Webb Hayes.*

The Hayes' entertaining style at the White House was more casual than in the past. Mrs. Hayes had no grown daughters, but was assisted by her nieces, cousins, and daughters of friends. It was reported that these young ladies had helped enliven the White House. Mrs. Hayes was the first President's wife to be called the "First Lady" by the Washington press.

Not only was President Hayes' election disputed, but also other elected government officials' elections were challenged. When newly elected La Fayette Grover of Oregon took his seat in the Senate on March 4, documents challenging his election were presented, signed by citizens of Oregon. The charges were that he had won the election by bribery and fraud. The charges were referred to a three-man committee of Senators to go to Oregon and investigate. The committee was made up of Senator Morton as chairman, with Senator Samuel J. R. McMillan and Senator Eli Saulsbury.

Lucinda and Morton, along with President Hayes and other politicians and leaders of society in Washington, traveled to Louisiana to attend the wedding of ex-Governor Henry Warmoth. This trip was soon after their second son, Walter, had graduated from the Pennsylvania Military Academy in Chester, Pennsylvania. Walter did so well in his studies of civil engineering that he graduated at the head of his class. He gave the valedictorian address at his graduation. Walter was hired by Captain Eads to work on the jetties at the mouth of the Mississippi River. Jetties are structures that project from land out into the river, and may be a breakwater or a walkway built as a means of constricting a channel.

The trip to Oregon was scheduled for early June. On Decoration Day, at the end of May 1877, Morton gave his last speech in Indianapolis at Crown Hill Cemetery. Civil War veterans, their families, and others gathered to honor the fallen heroes. In his speech, Morton said, "We come here today, soldiers and fellow citizens, to spread flowers upon the graves of these fallen heroes, to show our love for the cause for which they died and our gratitude to them for their sacrifice. And we ought to continue to do this as long as we live."

The tradition of laying flowers on graves started before the Civil War ended. Grieving family and friends began placing flowers on the graves of fallen soldiers as a way to honor them. A special day was designated for this and was called Decoration Day. This observance evolved into a yearly commemoration, honoring all military personnel who died in American wars. In 1971, the day was changed to a weekend observance, and Memorial Day was established as a legal holiday on the last Monday in May.

## A Trip to Oregon

On June 7, the Senator Grover Election Investigating Committee left Indianapolis for Portland, Oregon. Morton was feeling weak. He was given a special place on the train to recline and rest while traveling. His companions were Senator Saulsbury and his niece; Mrs. Morton; former Governor John Burbank and his mother, Mrs. Burbank;

D. S. Alexander, clerk; and C. N. Stagg, phonographer (a person who can write shorthand for recording speech). Senator McMillan would join them at Omaha. Ollie (Oliver T.), Morton's youngest son, also joined the party at some point.

It was the duty of the Senate Committee on Privileges and Election, of which Morton was chairman, to examine the facts and question witnesses about the accusations of fraud in the election of Senator Grover. On the long trip to San Francisco, Morton was unable to do much but lie on his couch. At San Francisco, the party boarded a ship to Portland. The voyage and the sea air seemed to revive Morton and he felt much better by the time they arrived. He was not to be talked out of this journey, and Lucinda must have been very worried about him. Since the beginning of the year, Morton had struggled to feel well enough to meet his obligations for what he felt was his duty.

The Grover investigation lasted eighteen days. The long, grueling days of interviewing over one hundred and fifty witnesses wore everyone out. Morton outworked them all, leaving the party exhausted when they were finished. Along with the work of the committee, Morton prepared an elaborate political speech he intended to give in Ohio when they returned. At the end of the investigation, Morton gave a long speech at a public meeting in Salem, Oregon. The newspapers declared it was the "best speech ever given in Oregon." This was Morton's last public speech.

## Morton's Last Journey

Morton, Lucinda, and Ollie traveled back to San Francisco in early August. On the night of August 6, they were entertained at the home of a prominent citizen and returned to their hotel between nine and ten o'clock p.m. Morton ate a rather heavy snack, and then retired. About midnight, he woke and told Lucinda that he felt weak. He could not get up or walk across the room, something he had been able to do without help. Lucinda woke their son and they helped him up to try to move around. After an hour or so, he complained that he was losing the use of his left arm, and by morning, his entire left side was paralyzed.

Morton's condition was alarming. After the grueling session in Oregon, he had seemed fairly well and there had been no warning signs of something amiss. Refusing to let his condition stop them, he insisted that they start home the next day. A special car was prepared for him with a bed and the best arrangements possible for his comfort. He was quite depressed and thought he might not live through the journey. Although Morton tried to endure his illness with little complaining, Lucinda understood how sick he was. After a couple of days on the train, it was too much for her and young Oliver to handle. They sent word to Will Holloway, their brother–in-law, to meet them at Cheyenne, Wyoming Territory. At Peoria, Illinois, Morton's longtime physician, Dr. W. C. Thompson, joined them.

The Indianapolis house was not prepared to receive the severely ill man, so the party continued on to Richmond, Indiana, to the home of Lucinda's mother. Mrs. Burbank lived with her son John after her husband died. The Morton party arrived in mid-August. The house was at 115 North Twelfth Street, the fourth house north of North A Street. The house was spacious and Morton and his family would be able to stay there while he recuperated. His room was on the lower floor in the

*The John Burbank home in Richmond, Indiana. Morton returned here after his stroke in California.*

front where he could look across the street to the peaceful churchyard of the Hicksite Quaker church, now the Wayne County Historical Museum. It was much quieter than his home in Indianapolis, and it was hoped that the fresh air, shady trees, and tranquil view would help him to return to health.

Morton was given every consideration during his stay in Richmond and the best of medical care. He received constant and loving care from his wife. Will Holloway, Sarah Gill, Rachel Scott, John Burbank, and Mrs. Burbank helped with anything they could. As soon as it was known of his illness, the newspapers all over the country carried stories on Morton's progress. Although he was very ill, his family and friends did not think it would be fatal. Many newspapers gave daily updates about his health. One article would report he seemed to be getting better, but the next report might say he was worse.

Almost immediately, Morton and the family began receiving letters and telegrams of encouragement from all over the country. He had visitors nearly every day from friends and many political colleagues. Although he suffered from pain and the hot Indiana weather, his visitors were greeted with as much good cheer as he was able to give. But they could see that he was very ill.

Morton tried to be optimistic about his recovery. He tried to assure his family and associates that he would be well enough to attend the next session of Congress. Morton was completely paralyzed except for his right arm, which he could move a bit. He lost considerable weight and his features were pinched with pain. He could not digest anything but a little milk or beef broth. The paralysis had affected his stomach and it was hard for him to swallow. It was difficult for him to speak clearly. Advice to help him, as many as six letters a day, began arriving to offer help for his stomach problems.

President Hayes had a scheduled visit to Dayton, Ohio in early September. Mrs. Hayes stayed in Dayton, while the President and his party then took a special trip to Richmond to see Morton. Although it was not an official visit to Richmond, crowds of cheering people met him at the train station at 9:30 a.m. and welcomed him. President Hayes' visit to Morton was brief because of Morton's weakness and inability to rise from his bed. When Hayes arrived, he found Lucinda and her brother John Burbank, sitting with Morton and reading to him. The doctor agreed the President could visit for a short time. Morton had been very despondent and depressed because of his slow recovery.

President Hayes' cheerful presence seemed to rally Morton and he greeted his visitor warmly. He thanked the President for coming and assured him that he would be in his seat at the next session of the Senate to support the President's policies.

The President was shocked at how the robust man was broken, emaciated, and almost helpless. Hayes' visit was brief and when he left, the President leaned over and kissed his cheek. Although he kept his emotions in check, as soon as he left, President Hayes began to shed tears, for he knew he would probably never see his friend alive again. The President's party returned to the Richmond train station for the trip back to Ohio. Again, thousands gathered along the streets and at the station to get a glimpse of the President. It was a rare occasion when the President of the United States visited Richmond. The party was back in Dayton by noon, where Mrs. Hayes joined them. The President's party immediately left for Fremont for the reunion of his old regiment the next day.

After Hayes left the Burbank house, a family member spoke to the group of reporters that had gathered outside. Although it was early in the day, they were asked to leave so that Morton and his family could have some quiet and rest—and the reporters respected the request.

Morton seemed to be a little better. Hayes' visit gave him hope and his spirits improved. Lucinda left for Indianapolis to make arrangements for his return to their home. On the evening of October 15, Morton was placed aboard the private train car of Colonel J. F. Miller for the trip to Indianapolis. The short trip seemed to revive his spirits and raised his hopes for a full recovery. He tried to take as little medicine as he could, but the pain was so severe that he could only find relief through strong doses of morphine. Every possible remedy was tried, and on at least one occasion, the doctor used bloodletting (withdrawal of blood from a patient for therapeutic purposes) to see if that would help. Bloodletting was still being used but fell out of favor by many doctors by the early 20th century.

Nothing really helped Morton's situation and he grew weaker and weaker. He tried to distract himself by having family members read the newspapers to him, especially the political news. Even through his pain and suffering, his mind stayed clear, and he was uncomplaining. Soon, he stopped asking to be read to and rarely spoke. His strong will was worn out and he continued to decline. One day, when Lucinda was quietly moving around the room, he took her hand and spoke to those in the room, "In all these years of sickness, she never failed me."

During the final few days, his family was in constant attendance. Not long before he died, a friend tried to get Lucinda to rest and said, "You are doing too much." She replied, as though it had never crossed her mind, "Doing too much? I am doing nothing. I would gladly die for him."

Lucinda had rarely left his side during all the months of his last illness. His sons Walter and Ollie, his brothers-in-law, Lucinda's sisters, and close friends stayed by his bedside as his life faded away. On the afternoon of November 1, 1877, Ollie asked him, "Father, do you know me?" He nodded that he did. As each of his family members kissed him, he acknowledged that he knew them. A few minutes after five o'clock, Dr. Thompson was holding his hand when Morton said, "I am dying; I am worn out." A few minutes later, he breathed his last.

The long deathwatch was over. Lucinda put her arms around her sons and said, "My darling boys." They were left alone with Morton for a few minutes to say their farewells in private. Their oldest son, John, had not been able to come to his father's side. They had received word that he was seriously ill in Alaska. Morton was not told of John's illness so as not to add worry to his pain. It was some time before John came back to San Francisco and learned of his father's death.

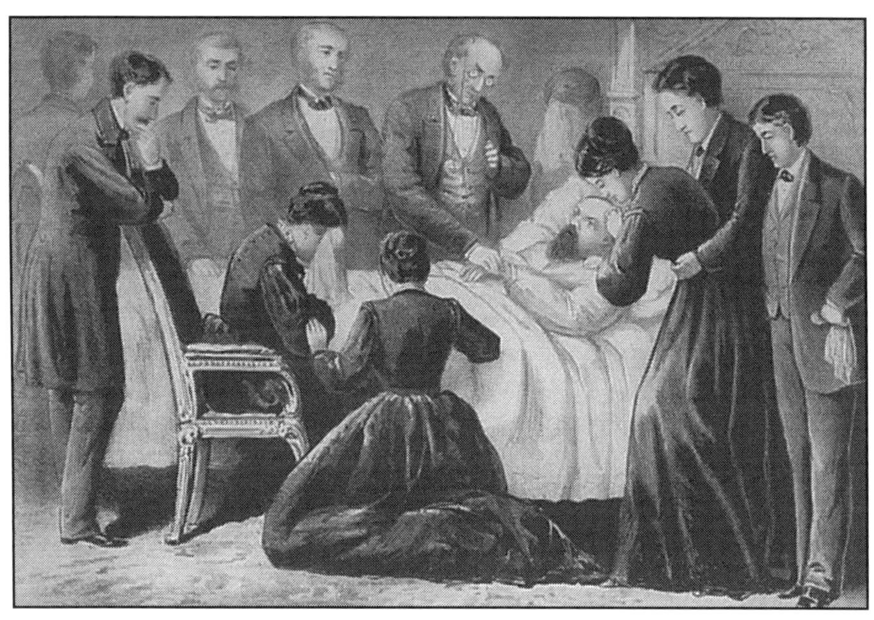

*(Above) Death of Oliver P. Morton with family gathered. Lucinda is on the chair at the end of the bed, circa 1877. Currier and Ives print.*

*(Right) Oliver Morton's bedroom and parlor after his death at his Indianapolis home. Courtesy of The Indiana Album: Joan Hostetler Collection.*

Word of Senator Morton's death spread across the nation. His condition had been news for several months, and although his death was expected, it still came as a shock. By order of the President, flags were lowered to half-staff on government buildings. Newspapers reported that the grief of the country seemed nearly as great as at the death of President Lincoln. Morton had traveled all throughout the states, from east to west, north and south, and as far as Oregon and California. Large crowds of people had attended his speeches or read them in the newspapers. He was the leader of the Republican Party and probably the most well-known Senator in Congress at the time.

The President and Vice President sent messages of condolences to the family. President Hayes' son attended the funeral in his place. The Senate and House of Representatives sent committees to attend the funeral. Government offices in many states were closed so officials could attend the funeral ceremonies. Memorial flowers and ornaments were sent to the house and letters and telegrams came from people who wanted to comfort the family.

The grieving public held meetings and passed resolutions in honor of Morton. In Indianapolis, many groups such as the bar association, organizations of colored men, Masons and The Odd Fellows Lodges, university students, letter carriers, and many others paid tribute to him. On the days of mourning in Indianapolis, fire bells were tolled fifty-four times—Morton's age, ringing morning, noon, and night until after the funeral was over. Black crepe was hung, and flags were lowered to half-staff. Indianapolis had never seen such large and elaborate funeral preparations for anyone.

Lucinda had held up as long as she could. She was so worn out that she became ill and was put to bed. Her sisters, Eliza Holloway, Rachel Scott, and Sarah Gill took care of her and the household duties. Her family had to finalize the funeral arrangements, and Will Holloway helped the boys do what needed to be done. Some funeral arrangements had been planned earlier when it became clear that he would not survive.

At the Morton house, the furnishings that had been rearranged for Morton's comfort were put back into place. The rooms were cleaned and prepared for family or guests who might come. Everyone who stayed by the sickbed was worn out with the long vigil as well as the grief they felt. Lucinda lay on her bed, almost comatose from the stress and lack of rest she went through while caring for her beloved husband. She was too ill to attend the funeral.

Morton's body was placed in a metallic casket and a military escort took it to the Marion County Courthouse where it was to lie in state from Sunday to Monday noon. Thousands of people passed by the remains, showing their respect and grief for Morton. About noon on Monday, the cortege and escorts took the casket to Roberts Park M. E. Church, a few blocks north on Delaware Street. All along the route, residents had hung flags and draped doors and windows in

*Oliver P. Morton's funeral cortege.*
*Courtesy of The Indiana Album: Joan Hostetler Collection.*

black crepe. At one house, a large portrait of Morton was hung with these words over the top, "Our Noble Senator."

The streets along the way were lined with hundreds of people. Special trains arrived, carrying people who wanted to view the body, attend the funeral, or take part in the long procession to the cemetery. Morton's family and friends filled most of the seats in the large church, and there was no more room for all the mourners. The quiet crowd waited outside to join the long parade to the cemetery.

The funeral began at 1:00 p.m. on Monday, November 5, 1877. Rev. J. B. Cleaver of the Central Christian Chapel, Mrs. Morton's church, conducted the services. The sermon was given by Rev. Joseph Bradford of the Roberts Park M. E. Church. He reviewed the Senator's life, character, and political career. The eulogy was given by Dr. J. H. Baylies, also of the Roberts Park M. E. Church. His focus was on the character of Morton as he knew him. Dr. Baylies was a personal friend and could speak from his own knowledge of the family. Much emphasis was given to Morton's generous and loving care toward his family and their love for each other.

Professor Samuel Hoshour, who had conducted their marriage ceremony in Centerville in 1845, offered the prayer. He was Morton's teacher at the Wayne County Seminary and his lifelong friend and advisor. Rev. Joseph F. Tuttle D.D., President of Wabash College in Crawfordsville, gave the benediction.

General Lew Wallace was in charge of the cemetery procession. Long lines of carriages, military troops, organizations, and mourners moved along the crowded streets north to Crown Hill Cemetery, nearly two miles away. Crown Hill Cemetery was officially dedicated in 1863, and in 1866, the federal government purchased 1.4 acres for a national cemetery in Crown Hill, and 700 Union soldiers who died in Indianapolis were moved to the new burial grounds. Oliver P. Morton was laid to rest in a plot where other members of the family were later interred.

The once strong, powerful, and persuasive voice was stilled at 54 years old. Lucinda and her sons must face the rest of their lives without his strong, loving, and guiding presence.

*Oliver Morton monument at Crown Hill Cemetery.*

# Part 4

# WIDOW MORTON

# Chapter 24

# LIFE WITHOUT OLIVER

It took a few weeks before Lucinda felt able to face the changes that Oliver's death made in her life. She put on her black mourning clothes and prepared to meet her obligations. So much had happened since he died that she was almost too busy to grieve. Walter went back to work in Mississippi and Ollie would be returning to Yale University. Their oldest son, John, had not been heard from for many months. He had been sent to the island of St. Paul, Alaska by the Alaska Seal and Fur Company, his employer. A steamer was sent for him in September

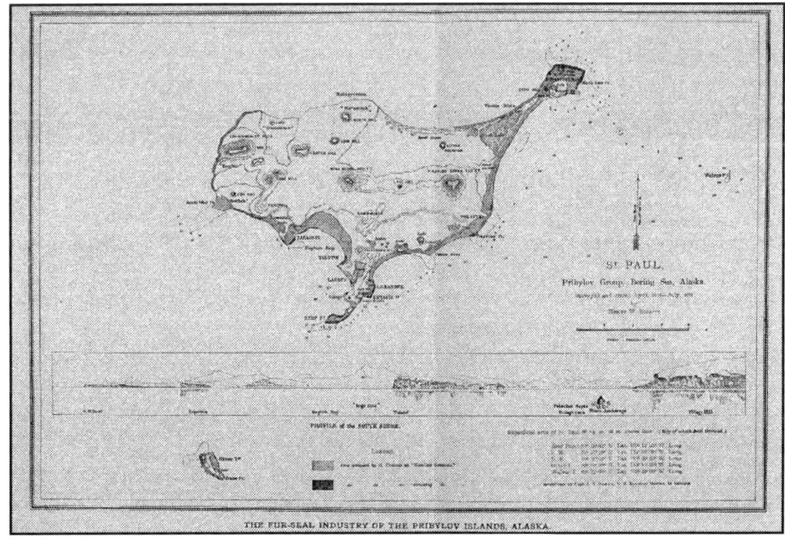


*An 1874 map of St. Paul Island, Alaska, created for the fur seal industry.*

1877, but he was too sick to be removed. His wife left the children with relatives in California and traveled on a steamer to meet him. She planned to stay with him on the island until he was well enough to come home.

Three attempts were made to bring them home. The first was in early winter, but the ice-floes prevented the ship from reaching the island. In March 1878, a new ship, the *General Miller*, was sent by the company, but soon after leaving port, it foundered and all on board perished. Finally, a third attempt was successful and the French schooner, *La Girondes*, was able to reach the island, and John and Hattie Morton were rescued from their long ordeal. On boarding the ship, John was told of his father's death. They returned to San Francisco in early August 1878, almost a year from the time John became ill and was out of touch. Word finally reached Lucinda, and it was met with great relief. There had been much concern that John may have died.

Shortly after the death of Senator Morton, several of his friends and admirers met in Indianapolis to plan a statue of him to be erected in the city. It was to commemorate his great service to the state and to the nation. The Morton Memorial Association was organized to carry out the plan with General Lew Wallace as president. Funds would be collected and the statue would be paid for by the association. On November 14, the Trustees of Crown Hill Cemetery donated a larger site next to Morton's grave for the family and as a possible place for the monument. The final place for the statue was chosen later.

Morton's estate was valued at about $50,000. The estate included a farm in White County, bank stocks, and one-half interest in *The Indianapolis Daily Journal*. Everything was left to Lucinda except for a few gifts to family. One of his main concerns was that sons Oliver T. and Walter complete their educations. Walter had graduated as a civil engineer in the spring of 1877, and was earning his own living in Mississippi. Gifts of specific books were given to his nieces and nephews. Lucinda's sisters, Sarah Gill, Rachel Scott, and her mother, Mary E. Burbank, were to "receive assistance as she, in her judgment, might think right." His thanks and regard went to brothers-in-law William Holloway and John Burbank for their kindness. Two other gifts of money were $100 given to Anna Maria Hart and $100 to Mrs. Abbie Caldwell. These two ladies may have been housekeepers or other employees of the Morton family.

As soon as Lucinda was able, Will Holloway and her brother John helped her with the process of settling the estate. Things that needed attention included acknowledging and answering the many letters and telegrams of condolence that were received by the family. Some were addressed to Lucinda and some were to William Holloway, who managed Morton's affairs while he was ill. Letters came from Senators, Representatives, Governors, officials of both parties in Congress, and politicians of both Republicans and Democrats in Indiana. Friends, admirers, veterans' organizations, and other groups sent their condolences. Several fresh floral offerings and symbolic pieces were sent to the home to be placed on the grave.

It was clear by the outpourings of sympathy how well beloved Oliver Morton was—in spite of all the bitter and hateful things printed by rival newspapers. A few letters of condolence sent to Mrs. Morton have been preserved. One was from the Colored Citizens of Owensboro, Kentucky. Chairman Henry McCrary, on their behalf, wrote,

> *We the Colored Citizens of Owensboro do desire to offer to Gov. Morton's family our friends, our warmest sympathy in this great affliction. Amid the general manifestations of sorrow at the public loss of which no one can be more sensible than we are that Gov. Morton was our friend and we do wish to be counted among those who feel in his death the grief of a personal bereavement.*
>
> *Chairman Henry McCrary*

A group of Colored Citizens of Philadelphia sent a floral anchor that was placed on Morton's grave. Men of colored organizations of Indianapolis marched in the procession to the cemetery. Morton, while in the Senate, was a bold and outspoken advocate of civil rights for former slaves and free Blacks.

Others that grieved for the loss of Morton's voice on their behalf were the organizations of woman suffrage. One letter of condolence sent to Lucinda expressed sorrow and comfort. The letter said:

> *In behalf of the friends of woman suffrage, Mrs. Francis Minor and myself present a slight token of the gratitude and respect we hold for Senator Morton—who so nobly vindicated our cause, in Senate Chambers and abroad. May it be counted worthy to crown with the many other more costly, yet none be less tender and true, the little hillock in yonder Cemetery, which shall mark the resting place of him, who goes to his long sleep, universally regretted.*
>
> *Very Sincerely,*
>
> *Phoebe W. Couzins of St. Louis*

The gift sent by these women was a broken column with flowers. The broken column was a common gift for the bereaved. It signified a life taken too early. The many floral and other tributes decorated Morton's grave after the funeral. They included a shield and floral pillow from President and Mrs. Hayes. Several broken columns, anchors, hearts, and a harp all covered with flowers. These were expensive tributes. The flowers would fade, but the more sturdy things like the broken columns would lay on the grave for a long time.

## Life Moves On

Lucinda moved forward with the plan for Oliver T. to complete his education at Yale. Oliver and his mother returned to New Haven, Connecticut. In 1879, she wrote in a letter to John that "it was desolate and that Ollie could not get into Yale without a tutor." They returned to Indianapolis. Oliver T. went back to Yale the next semester and his mother moved back to New Haven with him.

On June 18, 1879, son John Morton was appointed as the Consul of the United States at Honolulu, Oahu, and adjacent parts within the same allegiance. His credentials were sent to the King of the Hawaiian Kingdom, who accepted them. His family still resided in San Francisco.

Memories of Governor Oliver P. Morton were still strong in the minds of his friends. Whenever political comrades or friends of Morton were in Indianapolis, they made time to visit Lucinda. President Hayes stayed with her on one of his visits. She still resided in the same house for a time, and Sarah Gill and her daughter, Josephine, lived with her.

Eliza Holloway, Lucinda's sister, lived in Indianapolis with her husband, Will, and their son, Edward. Ollie, Edward, and Josephine, all cousins, were close companions. In 1881, Eliza, or Lida as the family called her, had been ill for some weeks when she took a turn for the worse and died in September. Lucinda was in New Haven with Ollie. Lucinda had the sad duty of writing her "darling sons" that their beloved aunt had died. Because of their close relationship, the boys often visited or stayed with Lida and Will Holloway when their parents were away.

When Oliver finished his studies at Yale, plans were made for him to attend Oxford University in London. This had probably been planned before his father died. Oliver T. enrolled in the University of Oxford for the winter term of 1881–1882. The University is made up of several colleges. Oliver T. attended the Christ Church College. Lucinda went with him to England and stayed during the first session. For his summer break, Oliver T. traveled to Germany where he took some classes at a German University. Lucinda came home in the spring of 1882 and returned to England later that year.

Lucinda had many acquaintances in London and was received in the best English society. She attended functions of the nobility where she met European statesmen and authors. She became friends with Max Müller, the German writer and Sanskrit scholar, and his wife. She spent several more months with her son and returned to the United States in June 1883.

In the meantime, son Walter had moved from Mississippi to St. Paul, Minnesota. In October 1881,Walter wrote a letter to "My Darling Mother," asking about the family and telling that he would not be able to be with her in the winter. He was working on a new project for the city that would bring him a substantial payment. He spoke of Lucinda going to see John, Hattie, and the children. Throughout the letter, he spoke warmly of Ollie and John and the death of his Aunt Lida.

Walter was the chief engineer on projects in St. Paul. He was described as being highly esteemed, with a straightforward character and a genial manner. Even though he was still quite young, his reputation as a civil engineer grew, and he was connected with some of the most important and difficult engineering projects in the country. Walter met his bride, Susan Thompson, in St. Paul, and they were married there on September 20, 1882.

During the summer, Lucinda and her brother John Burbank exchanged lots in Martindale's Hill Place addition in Indianapolis. John had owned lots 4 and 5; Lucinda had owned lots 11 and 12. The lots had no buildings on them and it is not clear why the exchange was made. Lucinda often traveled to see her sons. Her name is mentioned in the newspapers when she returned, living in several different places, but not in Martindale's Hill Place. She rented out her large house while she was gone, often for months at a time.

## The Circle Monument

The plans for the Morton monument were progressing and the statue was to be cast in bronze. The arrangements for the Morton

Memorial Association Statue had stalled for a time. Lew Wallace gave up his leadership when he became the Territorial Governor of New Mexico from September 1878 to March 1881. Colonel William M. Dudley was president for a short time. When an epidemic of yellow fever broke out, fundraising stopped for a year and a half. Colonel Dudley resigned when he was appointed Commissioner of Pensions at Washington, D.C. Ex-Governor Conrad Baker was then made president of the association. He initiated new efforts to raise enough money so that sculptors could present their ideas for the statue. The commission for the statue was given to the sculptor Franklin Simmons.

Franklin Simmons was a prominent American sculptor. He moved his home and studio to Rome in 1868, but returned several times to the United States. His first suggestion was that Morton be dressed in a classic Roman toga, but it was decided that he should be depicted in modern clothing. In July 1883, Lucinda traveled to Rome to see the clay model and to give her suggestions to the artist. She was able to travel to Rome since she was still living in England with Oliver T. at the time.

According to *The Indianapolis Journal*, "After a critical inspection of the work, she accorded it her unqualified commendation and preparations were entered upon for the casting of the bronze. It was cast in Rome to the entire satisfaction of the artist." The statue arrived in Indianapolis on November 21, 1883, duty free—without import or other taxes.

Additional funds for the project were still being collected, mostly \$1 to \$2 from individuals, and some gave \$10 to \$15. Towns and counties collected larger amounts. A concert to benefit the monument fund was given on December 21 at Lyra Hall and raised a substantial amount. At the time of the unveiling, there was still a need for \$100 to \$150. By mid-February, all funds had been collected.

The pedestal was set up, and on January 10, 1884, the statue was placed upon it. The statue was wrapped, and before the unveiling, it would be covered with large American flags. The artist came to

Indianapolis to supervise the process.

The day of unveiling was on January 15, 1884. Grand Army posts from all over the state were invited to march in the parades and attend the unveiling service at the English's Opera House. The many veterans' groups and others formed a long parade as they walked to the theater for the unveiling ceremony. Those attending from the Grand Army posts were seated on the main floor and invited guests and speakers were on the stage. Boxes in the surrounding galleries held distinguished guests. Box No. 1 held the theater owner, William H. English's family. He had given the use of the theater at no cost. Box No. 2 seated Lucinda; her sisters, Mrs. R. E. Scott, of Richmond and Mrs. S. C. Gill, of Indianapolis; Oliver T. Morton; Mrs. John Newman; and Mrs. John M. Morton and two children, of San Francisco. Lucinda's son John was not able to attend with his family and Walter was not able to come because of the illness of his partner. Several other boxes held other family members, friends, and dignitaries. After the speeches, another parade formed for the trip to the Circle Park for the unveiling of the statue.

As the crowd gathered and surrounded the Circle, Governor Albert Porter and former Governor Baker, holding a bright looking little boy by the hand, mounted the temporary stand by the side of the statue. Former Governor Baker addressed the crowd saying, "The duty has been devolved upon me of unveiling the statue. I have taken the right to delegate that duty to another, the little boy, nine years old, the son of John M. Morton of San Francisco, who is the eldest son of Senator Morton, to Oliver P. Morton, the grandson of the great statesman."

Young Oliver P. Morton pulled the cords. Two large American flags fell apart uncovering the bronze statue of the late war Governor, patriot, and statesman. As the flags fell, the band struck up the song, "Hail Columbia." Rev. David Walk delivered the prayer that closed the ceremony.

Indiana Senator Benjamin Harrison was in attendance at the monument unveiling. At the time of the event, he suggested that another monument and statue to all the soldiers of Indiana be erected as a companion piece to the Morton monument. The suggestion was taken up immediately and acted upon. This monument would be one of which every citizen of the state could be proud. Since the Grand Army was already organized with posts in every part of Indiana, it was proposed that they should carry out the plans. The first gift of $50 to start the fund was given by the *Terre Haute Courier* newspaper. The planned monument would turn out to be a much larger and grander project than first suggested.

*Circle Park, Indianapolis. The Oliver P. Morton statue, placed there in 1884, stands at the lower lefthand corner. Courtesy of Indiana Historical Society.*

# Chapter 25

# OLIVER THROCK MORTON

Oliver T. finished his time at Oxford in 1884 without graduating. It did not seem as important to graduate as to have attended the college classes. He returned to Indianapolis and began studying law with an established lawyer. He also followed in his father's footsteps by making speeches on behalf of the Republican Party. His first political speech was in 1884 at the Blaine and Logan Club in Noblesville at the beginning of the fall election campaign. According to the report, "The main courtroom was 'crowded to overflowing' to hear the son of the great Senator Morton speak." Oliver T. was soon making speeches all over the state. This continued throughout the fall and he was often given first place in the advertisements. The events drew large crowds to hear him. Oliver T. never ran for political office, but was a very vocal supporter of the Republican Party in Indiana and the nation.

Not long after returning home from England, Lucinda spent a few weeks with John's family in California. She returned in September. When Lucinda was in Indianapolis, she did not remain in retirement. She attended church and helped with other activities. In the fall of 1885, there were plans made to have a military carnival with an exhibit of military relics from past wars. The committee was organized by the State Librarian, Miss Lizzie O. Callis. She asked Lucinda to be a member and help set up the Museum and Relics exhibit.

This winter carnival turned out to be a large hit in spite of the cold weather. There were events the last week of February. The military exhibits, concerts, and dances were held the week of March 10. Thousands of people from around the state attended. The last night was the military ball. Five thousand invitations were sent, and it was a huge success.

The society pages took note of Lucinda's activities. Her lunches, teas, and parties were reported as part of the Indianapolis "society." Guests to her home included family, as well as people such as Robert M. Burns, superintendent of the Pullman Works. Ex-President Hayes stayed with her in November 1885, for the funeral of Vice President Thomas Hendricks. Hendricks was a former Governor of Indiana and had served as Vice President under Grover Cleveland.

*Oliver T. Morton was the featured speaker at the Park Theater, Indianapolis, as seen in this advertisement in the October 11, 1884 "Indianapolis Journal."*

Oliver T. was making a name for himself by working with and writing for *The Indianapolis Journal*. *The Indianapolis Times Company* was purchased by *The Journal* and it was renamed *The Indianapolis Times*, a morning paper. It was incorporated in January 1886, with directors Oliver T., William R. Holloway, and Edward Holloway. The newspaper was not successful and closed in about seven months. In August 1886, *The Indianapolis Journal Newspaper Publishing Company* was incorporated and it absorbed the *Indianapolis Times*. Oliver T. stayed with the paper as part owner with new partners. William Holloway and his son,

Edward, evidently did not stay in the business.

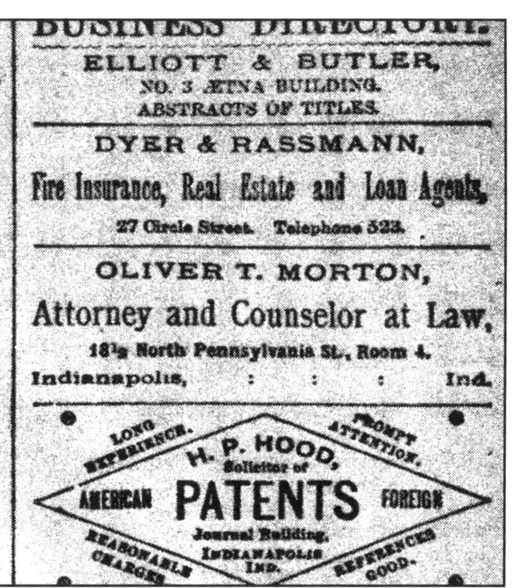


*An advertisement for Oliver T. Morton, Attorney and Counselor at Law, Indianapolis, in an 1888 edition of "The Indianapolis Journal."*

Oliver T. passed the bar in 1887 and opened his own office as Attorney and Counselor at Law. He was becoming a well-respected writer. He wrote several articles for the *Atlantic Monthly* and was praised for his essays on political subjects.

Lucinda spent several weeks with her sons when she visited them. She visited John's family in San Francisco and Walter's in St. Paul, Minnesota. Walter's first child, a daughter, was born in 1887. John had a son and daughter. When not traveling or visiting family and friends, Lucinda stayed involved with local events. She supported the women's suffrage movement and was active in charities and on committees. Her name often appeared in the social columns.

Lucinda had lived in several places in Indianapolis since her husband's death. In 1887, she purchased a house in Woodruff Place. She resided there with her sister, Sarah and her daughter.

Lucinda's sons had not been together with their mother for over ten years. In February 1889, the three sons visited Lucinda at her home at Woodruff Place. Their picture was taken at the time and it is the last one of Lucinda with her sons. This would be the last time they would all be together before death would separate them.

*Lucinda Morton, center, and her sons (left to right), John Miller Morton, Walter Scott Morton, Oliver Throck Morton, circa 1889. Courtesy of Walter Morton descendants, the Santarelli de Brasch family.*

In 1889, it had been twelve years since Governor Morton died. Every year since his death, he was remembered. There were church services and other memorial gatherings of Civil War veterans. On November 6, a Carrara marble bust of Morton was placed upon a temporary pedestal at his gravesite in Crown Hill. Franklin Simmons, who was the sculptor for the Circle Park monument, made the bust. In spite of the cold weather, several members of the Morton family attended, along with a large number of veterans, groups of ladies, and others. They came to hear again the eulogies of the Great War Governor and remember the last speech he gave here, not long before his own death.

Often when Lucinda returned to Indianapolis, she would visit Oliver's grave. On one visit to the cemetery in 1900, she found several old soldiers at the grave looking at the monument. They did not know who she was, and when learning that she was the widow, they shared with her their memories of Morton and how he had taken care of them.

Memorial tributes continued to be held for Governor Morton throughout the state of Indiana, usually on Memorial Day in May, or in November. Lucinda received letters and copies of programs from other places. She would write back and thank the writer for the tribute and for sending her a program.

Other tributes to the Governor continued, such as schools and city streets around Indiana being named for him. In 1890, a new school, School No. 29, was built at 2101 North College Avenue in Indianapolis. It was later given the name Oliver P. Morton School. The school was for children from first to eighth grade and was used for many years.

*School No. 29, the Oliver P. Morton School, in Indianapolis. It held classes for Grades 1 to 8, and is now closed. From the author's collection.*

The following July 1890, John was appointed Shipping Commissioner at San Francisco by the Secretary of the Treasury. His appointment was not without controversy. Some who disapproved accused the secretary of favoring him because of his father. All three sons were active in the Republican Party in the states where they were living. They all followed their father, Oliver P., in their ability to make speeches. Even with their high interest in politics, none sought public office.

Oliver T. had done very well in his Indianapolis law practice and as a speaker and writer. A new United States Court of Appeals for the Southern Illinois District was organized in 1891. Judge H. W. Blodgett of Indianapolis was assigned to be the judge of the court and Oliver T. Morton of Indiana was appointed Clerk of the District Court. His cousin, Edward Holloway, was appointed deputy clerk under him in 1894. Oliver moved to Chicago for his new job.

## Death of Josephine Gill

Josephine Gill, only daughter of Lucinda's younger sister, Sarah Gill, was a beloved niece of Lucinda. She, Edward Holloway, and Oliver T. were first cousins, close in age and close friends. At times, Oliver T. escorted her to social events in Indianapolis. Josephine had spent much of her life living in Richmond. She and her mother came to live with Lucinda after she purchased the house in Woodruff Place, a neighborhood in Indianapolis, about one mile east of downtown.

In December 1891, Sarah Gill, Josephine's mother, became violently ill on New Year's Eve. It was reported that only the skill of several physicians saved her from death. For some strange reason, Josephine died suddenly. The newspaper reported that "the strain was too much upon the young girl (Josephine) and her bright light was snuffed out." The cause of her death was given as "congestion of the brain." She was twenty-four years old.

Josephine had shown promise as a writer, like Oliver T. She was described as beautiful and charming and a "distinct addition to Indianapolis social and intellectual life." She was intelligent and already her work had been published in *The Century Magazine*. Her death was a terrible shock to the family, for she had died so suddenly while her mother was ill. Her funeral was held on January 4, 1892, at Lucinda's home in Woodruff Place. It was private, with only relatives and a few friends present. At the end of the service, Rev. Dr. Daniel R. Lucas, minister of the Christian Church, who had conducted the funeral, read one of Josephine's poems.

# Chapter 26

# CHANGING FORTUNES

During the years after her husband's death, Lucinda made trips to Europe and visited friends in New York and Washington. She made the long train rides to California and to Minnesota. Travel was expensive and she seemed to have an adequate income from various investments. The cost of her travels, Oliver T.'s school expenses, and buying a new house, made quite a dent in her income. Lucinda loaned son John money to buy land in California for a vineyard. He wrote to her telling that he would surely pay it back and had even put it in his will in case he died before it was paid.

After the Civil War, the financial climate of the country began recovering from the huge cost of the war. The era later known as the Gilded Age began about 1877 and lasted until the 1890s. It was a time of booming economy. Manufacturing and factories were expanding, and American wages grew higher. Railroads grew almost too fast and were a major investment for many. Mining, farming, and financial investments increased in importance.

Immigrants arrived in record numbers. From 1892 to 1954, the federal government operated a reception center on Ellis Island for new immigrants when they arrived. Each person had to pass a medical inspection before they could enter the U.S. There were limited facilities on the island to help people recover from temporary illnesses. Ellis

Island was close to the Statue of Liberty, a symbol of welcome to immigrants, that was erected in 1886. The Statue of Liberty was a Centennial gift from France for the 100$^{th}$ anniversary of the United States.

In October of 1892, Houghton, Mifflin & Co. published the book, *The Southern Empire* by Oliver T. Morton. According to the advertising, *The Southern Empire* was a collection of his essays on the probable effect on the Western world in a successful conclusion of the Southern rebellion.

At the end of 1892, an advertisement had been placed in the *Indianapolis Journal*. It was a Statement of Condition for the *Indianapolis Journal* newspaper. Oliver T. was part owner of the paper, as well as an editorial writer. The amount of the capital stock was $150,000; the amount of indebtedness was $18,103.92. Oliver T. Morton, Vice President, signed the statement. Oliver T. and Henry S. New were the directors. It seemed to be on sound financial foundation.

A financial collapse in the United States hit on Friday, May 6, 1893. Europe and other countries, because of their own financial difficulties, had been cashing in their American stocks, bonds, and paper money for specie—either gold or silver coin. It put such a strain on the American banks and the government that there was a "Panic of 1893." People withdrew their funds as quickly as they realized what was happening, causing banks to close. Wages dropped, agricultural crops and manufactured goods could not be shipped, and the whole country suffered. Many investors lost their money and were bankrupt. In spite of the financial disasters for banks, the full impact did not fully hit until several months later. No doubt, Lucinda's income took a hit along with everyone else. Oliver T. had a good job in Chicago and he helped her financially.

A grand fair was planned for that same year. It was The Columbian Exposition, held to celebrate the 400$^{th}$ anniversary of Christopher Columbus' arrival in the New World in 1492. It was also called the Chicago World's Fair. Earlier in the year, plans were made for a suffrage congress to be held during the World's Fair. Its purpose was to discuss a wide range of issues concerning the right to vote. William D. Foulke (biographer of Oliver P.) and Oliver T. Morton were on the planning committee. The event was to be held at the Arling Institute—not on the fairgrounds. The conference would consider the topic of who should be extended the right to vote—women and communities having mixed races, such as Blacks, Native Americans, and Chinese. There would be discussion about property or educational tests and other hindrances for citizens to vote. Another controversial subject, as to whether to abolish the Electoral College, would be debated. Oliver T. was one of the featured speakers.

During the summer of 1893, the Soldiers' Monument was back in the news. When Lucinda learned that the Morton Statue on the Circle was to be relocated, she was very upset. She asked Oliver T. to explain her position. The monument to Morton had been on the Circle for less than ten years. Oliver T. and his mother presented their objection to the Board of Regents who was making the decisions about the move. The Board of Regents was made up of veteran soldiers who revered the memory of Governor Morton and did not want to offend anyone. Although the statue would have to be moved, the Regents were trying to be sure it was done in a respectful way.

Oliver T. and Lucinda printed a circular that was widely distributed to the GAR (Grand Army of the Republic) posts and the newspapers. It was Lucinda's letter to the Board of Regents outlining her objections to moving the statue. After much discussion and compromise, the family's objections were satisfied. It was decided that the statue would only be moved from twelve to fifteen feet north of its present position. Two thousand dollars was allowed for the cost of the new pedestal, and it would take the entire amount to pay for the work. Oliver T. asked that he be allowed to design plans for the statue's pedestal and pay for it himself. He submitted a design by sculptor C. P. Atwood of Chicago, and it was approved.

Oliver T. found time to be in Indianapolis to work at the newspaper, although his main job was during the sessions of the Appeals Court in Chicago. He also helped with the relocating of his father's statue. Circle Park was enlarged to accommodate the large memorial building, and the cornerstone was laid on August 22, 1889.

Lucinda lived with Oliver T. in Chicago at different times, some for more than a year. She and Sarah had moved there in 1892. They were in the city during the time of the 1893 Chicago World's Fair and the suffrage conference, and no doubt, attended both. The fair was so large that visitors often returned several times to take it all in.

Lucinda returned to Indianapolis in April 1895, staying for a time at the Bates House Hotel. She planned to stay in Indianapolis, but her home had been rented and she could not move back until it was vacated.

Oliver T. had a good income from the newspaper and his position as Clerk of the Circuit Court. But in 1894, he brought suit in federal court to recover $371.20 that he had paid "under protest" to the Treasury Department. His claim stated that he was entitled to $3,000, his salary as clerk, but he had expenses of his office that were not reimbursed. He asked for a salary increase to $3,500, which was the salary of other clerks in his position. He won his action for recovery of the $371.20 and the salary raise, but it was protested by a district attorney who declared he should only have the original salary of $3,000.

Lucinda planned to stay in Indianapolis, but in May of 1896, she had to return to Chicago. The trip was earlier than she had planned because of the illness of Oliver T. He had health issues for quite a while, but he seemed to recover after each illness. He carried a lot of responsibility in his various jobs as well as being the one to look after Lucinda's interests.

At nearly the same time as the Soldiers' Monument was being built, another statue of Oliver P. Morton was in the planning stages for Washington, D.C. A new building in the capital had been built in 1819 for the House of Representatives. Although it was splendid and imposing, the acoustics promoted annoying echoes and made it difficult to hear and conduct business. A new hall was authorized in 1850. The House moved into its present chamber in the new House wing in 1857. The older hall stood empty for a time until it was decided to use it as an art gallery. In 1864, Congress invited each state to contribute two statues of prominent citizens for permanent display. The hall was renamed the National Statuary Hall.

## The Statue in Washington, D.C.

In the spring of 1892, the Indiana Legislature appointed a committee to plan for the erection of the statue of Oliver P. Morton in Statuary Hall, Washington, D.C. The committee members were State Senator Charles E. Shiveley of Richmond, Oliver T. Morton of Chicago, and Addison C. Harris of Indianapolis. The amount appropriated for the work was $5,000. In September, they contracted sculptor Charles H. Niehaus of New York, to make clay models. Two models were prepared, one of Morton in a sitting position and the other in the attitude of making a public address.

Niehaus was a well-respected artist. Two of his marble statues were already in Statuary Hall. They were of William Allen and James A. Garfield, both United States Senators from Ohio. In February 1898, the artist brought his clay models of Morton to Indianapolis. Oliver T. and Addison Harris viewed the models in Harris' office. After rejecting the seated model, Oliver T. had the standing model turned around slowly. Studying it carefully, he said, "Yes, that is Father."

The statue was to be made of the finest Italian marble, and with the pedestal, would stand eleven feet high. The statue was seven feet, from sole to crown, and the pedestal four feet tall. The finished work shows Morton as he might have been from age forty-five to fifty. He is dressed in a suit such as he wore.

Several books and essays have been written about Governor Morton since his death. One that would stand out above all others of the time was the two-volume *Life of Oliver P. Morton, Including His Important Speeches*, by William Dudley Foulke, published in 1899. It took nearly ten years in the writing. Oliver T. had taken a great interest in the memorials to his father. His opinion was sought for the statues and he consulted with Foulke about the biography. Both Oliver T. and Lucinda were well acquainted with Foulke and were able to give him personal information about their family. Lucinda and William Holloway had kept letters and documents from the time when Oliver P. was Governor and Senator. Having access to papers and family members made the books about Oliver P. Morton a reliable source of study about his life.

*William Dudley Foulke, author of "Life of Oliver P. Morton." Among other accomplishments, he was one of the early presidents of the American Woman Suffrage Association.*

## Death of Oliver T. Morton

Lucinda received a telegram on the morning of October 12, 1898, telling her that Oliver T. was very ill again. It was an urgent request for her to go to Chicago as quickly as possible. She left on the train at 3:35 that afternoon. In the early evening, Sarah Gill, Lucinda's sister, received a telegram stating that the young man had died. Oliver had not been well, but it did not seem life-threatening. This was a tragic blow for Lucinda, as her son was the youngest of five children. She had been his companion while he was at Yale and when he studied in England. She stayed with him in Chicago for months at a time and he would stay with her when he was in Indianapolis.

Lucinda and her nephew's wife, Mrs. Edward Holloway, accompanied the body from Chicago. Lucinda's other sons were able to come to the funeral. John was in Washington at the time, and Walter was in St. Paul. Other family members were in Richmond and Indianapolis. The funeral was held on October 14, at Lucinda's home at 140 East Drive, Woodruff. Friends were invited to the funeral, but the burial was private. His burial place is in Crown Hill Cemetery, near his father's grave. Shortly after her husband's death, Lucinda had the bodies of her two little girls moved from Centerville to the gravesite in Indianapolis. Now, three of her children were there with their father.

The death of Lucinda's youngest son was not only a personal grief to her, but it was shortly disclosed by his will that she would have no financial help from his estate. Even her home in Woodruff would be lost. *The Indianapolis Journal*, November 11, 1898 reported, "Mrs. Oliver P. Morton and her sister, Mrs. Gill, have vacated their Woodruff Place residence and taken apartments in the Ensley flats on West Vermont Street."

Oliver T. had never married and Lucinda was his sole beneficiary and the executor of his will. His assets did not cover the debts that he owed. He had not paid his rent for three months at the Metropolitan Hotel in Chicago where he lived. He had several other debts with very little savings. The details of the lawsuits brought against his estate were embarrassingly printed in the newspaper so that all could see.

The two-volume biography of Oliver P. Morton by Foulke has the copyright date of 1898, and it was published shortly after, in 1899. The dedication was "To the memory of Oliver T. Morton." Lucinda's friends were very concerned about her financial condition. Foulke and Bowen–Merrill Company, Indianapolis publishers, arranged to give Mrs. Morton all the profits from the sale of the biography in Indianapolis. This information was relayed to prospective readers, urging them to buy it. *The Indianapolis Journal* stated that the books should be in every library. "The literary style and the remarkable personality of which it treats combine to make it one of the most entertaining and desirable of biographies."

A week after Oliver T.'s death, his first cousin and close friend, Edward Holloway, was appointed to fill the position of the Clerk of the Court for the United States Circuit Court of Appeals in Chicago. Edward had been the Deputy Clerk for four years. His father, William Holloway, was the Consul General to St. Petersburg, Russia. The death of Oliver T. left Lucinda to cope with all the changes and difficulties. Her family, especially brother John Burbank, helped her through many problems. Her sister, Sarah Gill, lived with her and was her close friend and companion.

## Lucinda Receives a Pension

On January 20, 1899, Lucinda arranged to sell her late husband's library to the Indianapolis school board for $450. Lucinda's financial state was such a concern that it was brought to the attention of the Indiana State Legislature. On February 21, 1899, an act was passed by the Indiana General Assembly for the benefit of Mrs. Morton.

*An ACT making an appropriation to Lucinda M. Morton, widow of Oliver P. Morton, of One Hundred Dollars per month during her natural life.*

*H. 94. Approved February 21, 1899.*

While Lucinda's need for support was the main reason for the Act, the justification for this pension was Governor Oliver P. Morton's actions during the Civil War. He established and maintained an arsenal for the manufacture of ammunition. When the war was over, he kept nothing for himself, but turned over to the state all the funds after the loans were paid back. All the equipment and everything used at the arsenal were also turned over to the state. The total amount was the sum of $76,382.45. The interest on the money from that time added up to $25,000.

Because Lucinda, at age seventy-four, was in absolute need of financial aid for her daily subsistence, she was awarded $100 a month for life. The act took effect immediately. In the twenty-first century, it would be worth over $3,000 a month.

Only two of Lucinda's five children were still alive. She had suffered much grief and sorrow from the loss of loved ones. The publication of the new biography of her husband, and the many times she was asked to take part in memorials for him encouraged her. She was respected and honored for herself. The newspapers reported that Lucinda was invited to schools and clubs where she spoke of her husband's legacy. She presented a bust of him to the Oliver P. Morton School in Indianapolis.

When Lucinda had to give up her Woodruff home, she and Sarah moved into the former residence of Mr. May at No. 1411 Ash Street. This was temporary, for she later signed a one-year lease with Alice R. Charlton. The rent for the residence was $25 a month and it was located at 2215 Broadway Street in Indianapolis. The pension given by the State Legislature enabled Lucinda to live in relative comfort the rest of her life.

At the time the Washington statue was unveiled in January 1899, shortly before she was awarded the pension, critics of the statue derided the work as not portraying Morton as they remembered him. Those criticisms were aired in the newspapers. A Washington correspondent of *The New York Times* wrote, "The sculpture of Niehaus introduces the spectator to a man of more than average height, of very distinguished presence, of noble bearing, good clothes, and not a little self-consciousness. This makes a very interesting statue, but not a representation of Morton … As he appeared during the war to give a political speech, he was rather stooped-shouldered, somewhat careless about his dress, with a shock of hair quite unlike the trimmed suit shown on the statue, and a beard of quite different cut."

Addison C. Harris of Indianapolis, who was on the commission to arrange for the statue, penned a reply to the critics. He had known Governor Morton well and consulted with his son, Oliver T., on the clay models. His letter stated the facts of how the statue was designed.

"I was chairman of the committee appointed by Governor (James) Mount to provide for the statue … It was the purpose of the committee to have a statue of Governor Morton as he was when Governor of our state. It was this period of his life that he showed his sterling qualities, and it is as Governor that he is best remembered and most

*Oliver P. Morton statue in Statuary Hall, Capitol Building, Washington, D.C.*

revered by the people of Indiana."

The sculptor Niehaus was provided with pictures of Morton while he was Governor. Measurements of his clothing were found at the tailor's and furnished to the sculptor. He measured the cast of Morton's head and face at the time of his death. It was from this information that the clay models were made. When Oliver T. examined the models, he said, "Yes, yes, that is Father in his strength."

The statue of Oliver P. Morton for the National Statuary Hall in Washington was presented on March 24, 1900 to the House of Representatives. Lucinda Morton, Sarah Gill, and John's son, Oliver P. Morton, Jr., who had unveiled the first Morton statue in Indianapolis, were seated in the crowded gallery reserved for Senator's families. Oliver T., who spent so much time serving on the statue committee, had died before the work was complete.

When the speeches were finished, the newspapers reported, "So affected was Mrs. Morton by the touching tribute by Senator Beveridge to the memory of him the world calls great, but who she remembers as her beloved, that the tears flowed from the fountain that not even time can exhaust. It was one of the most affecting sights ever witnessed in the Senate Chamber." The formal reception for the statue by the Senate was held on April 14.

On April 23 and 24, the annual convention of the Daughters of the American Revolution was held in New York City. Mrs. Oliver P. Morton represented the state of Indiana. In June, back home in Indianapolis, she gave the late Governor's carriage to the State Soldiers' Home. The old carriage had been cared for by G. H. Shove. He also shipped two brass guns and their carriages—the frame of mount to support the gun barrel, allowing it to be maneuvered and fired—to the Home. The items would be objects of interest to the "boys" and to visitors. In one of the gun wheels was found a mini ball, showing they were in actual service during the war.

## Death of Son, John Miller Morton

Word was received in late July that John Morton, Lucinda's oldest son, was seriously ill on St. Paul Island, in the Pribilof Islands. According to the description, the Pribilof Islands are a four-island archipelago in the Bering Sea, 300 miles from the Alaskan mainland. They were uninhabited until the late 1700s. Russia owned all the Aleutian Islands until a deal was made with the Americans to purchase them in 1867.

John Morton was appointed the Collector of Customs for the port of San Francisco in 1880. His home with his wife and two children was in San Francisco. He made trips to St. Paul Island to oversee the harvesting of fur seals. It was in 1877–1878 that John was ill and stranded on this same island with his wife for several months before he was rescued. Upon receiving word of John's latest illness, Senator Charles Fairbanks of Washington, D.C. immediately sent instructions to Captain Roberts of the revenue cutter *Manning*, at Nome City. He was to pick up John when they returned south in September.

By the time the ship reached St. Paul Island, John was dead. He died on July 15, 1900, and his grave was on the island of St. Paul. Dispatches from the small, isolated Pribilof Islands were slow to reach Washington. Secretary of the Treasury Lyman J. Gage received a telegram on August 15, telling him of John's death. John's friends in Washington had been very concerned since receiving word in July, and the newspapers recorded that Senator Fairbanks was untiring in sending whatever relief he could to the "stricken man."

The first report of John's sickness was that he suffered from locomotor ataxia. His death notice gave the cause of death as apoplexy. Apoplexy refers to stroke symptoms that occur suddenly, leading to death. John's father, Oliver P.; his grandfather, James; and Oliver's brother, William, all died as a result of illness due to stroke.

Lucinda was not at home in Indianapolis when word came of John's death. He was her oldest son, ten years older than his brother,

Walter, and fourteen years older than his deceased brother, Oliver T. John was very dear to Lucinda since he was her only living child for a time after the loss of her two baby daughters. Her two younger sons were very dear to her also, and she called them all her "darling boys."

John's body could not be brought home, so a symbolic funeral was held on September 21, in Indianapolis, at Lucinda's home on 2215 Broadway Street. Rev. Dr. Daniel R. Lucas, pastor of Lucinda's church, conducted the service. Friends and family attended it. Although there was no casket, there were honorary pallbearers. A private memorial was held in Crown Hill Cemetery at his father's grave.

# Chapter 27

# THE LAST YEARS

The magnificent Soldiers' and Sailors' Monument was finished in 1901. It was built on the enlarged Circle Park in Indianapolis and had taken thirteen years to complete. The monument's original purpose was to honor Hoosiers who were veterans of the American Civil War. However, it was decided that it should honor Indiana's soldiers who served in other wars from the American Revolution, Territorial conflicts with England and Spain, the War of 1812, the Mexican–American War, and the Spanish–American War. It was the first monument in the United States to honor the common soldier.

The monument's public dedication was on May 15, 1902. Several distinguished guests were seated on the platform. Among them were Governor Winfield Durbin of Indiana, Governor George Nash of Ohio, Mrs. Mary Harrison, wife of deceased ex-President Harrison, Mrs. Lucinda Morton, and her sister, Mrs. Sarah Gill. There were officers of the Armed Forces and representatives of veterans' organizations, as well as the beloved Indiana poet, James Whitcomb Riley.

Veterans of the Civil War that were able to take part carried their old regimental flags from the State House to the monument and placed the tattered remnants on display. Some men were so feeble that they had to stop and rest during the walk from the State House. The old veterans kissed the flags as they were placed. At the end of the ceremony, those aged veterans returned the flags to their keeper at the State House.

The chairman of the event was General Lew Wallace. Applause and cheers greeted Wallace, and he was nearly overcome by the response of the crowd. Lew Wallace was Indiana's distinguished statesman, soldier, and writer. *The Indianapolis Journal* reported, "Several minutes elapsed before he recovered the power of utterance. A thrill of sorrow ran through the audience as it became apparent that the noted Indianan was scarcely in physical condition to undertake the momentous duty of directing a great public ceremony … but his voice rang out with almost its old time power as he plunged into the heart of his vigorous and brilliant address."

There were several speeches and music by bands and choirs. When

*Dedication of Soldiers' and Sailors' Monument, Circle Park, Indianapolis in 1902. Courtesy of Indiana Historical Society.*

the band and flag bearers marched past the Morton statue, they dipped their colors in respect for the War Governor. When the American flag was raised over the monuments, a 700-voice men's choir sang "The Star Spangled Banner." The enthusiastic crowd cheered and applauded at every opportunity, sometimes so loud they drowned out the music or the speaker.

The principal speaker was Major E. W. Halford, who was secretary to Mr. Morton when he was in the Senate. He told many stories of the time he served Morton and praised the work he did in the Senate. One of his quotes about Morton was from Hon. W. I. Wilson of the U.S. Congress. He had attended Morton's funeral and stated, "No man would be thus mourned and buried who did not possess good qualities, both of head and heart."

The final and most anticipated speaker was James Whitcomb Riley. He composed a poem for the event called "The Soldier." Its solemn

*James Whitcomb Riley, Indiana's beloved poet.*

and sentimental verses spoken by the poet were received by the crowd with an ovation and cheers. The day continued with other ceremonies and celebrations. The newspapers declared this event drew the largest crowd that Indianapolis had ever seen.

Morton's original Circle statue was placed on the Northeast side of the Monument and three other statues are on each of the other three sides. They are James Whitcomb, Indiana's Governor from 1843–1848; George Rogers Clark; and William Henry Harrison, Indiana Territorial Governor.

The Soldiers' and Sailors' Monument is a tribute to those serving in wars from Indiana. The cost at the time of its construction was $600,000. In the twenty-first century, it would cost over 21 million dollars.

Lucinda's grandchildren in California were now grown. Her grandson had been with her for the dedication of the Morton statue in Washington. In January 1904, she received word that Mrs. John Morton's daughter, Harriet Mason Morton, had married Mr. John Barnett Hollen on December 9, 1903. They would be living in Sal Da Terra Row, Stanford University, Stanford, California.

That same year, Lucinda decided to build a house "on her lot in Indianapolis" at 616 East Twenty-First Street. In July, she contracted with J. W. Harrell to build a two-story house with basement. The house would have a bathroom, central heating with a furnace, and electric lighting. Lucinda and her sister Sarah would live there until Lucinda died in 1907.

In 1905, Lucinda celebrated her 80$^{th}$ birthday. She spent the day with family in Richmond. *The Indianapolis News* featured her picture and a story about her.

The article read:

*Mrs. Morton is one of the most distinguished women in Indiana. She is much beloved by her circle of friends for her charm of manner and graciousness. She is keenly alert to important questions of the day and is a great reader, keeping abreast of the daily papers and she reads many books. Recently in her reading she returned to historical subjects. Mrs. Morton last year designed her own plans and made all the business arrangements in building her new home at 616 East Twenty-first Street, this city, where she and her sister, Mrs. Gill live.*

INDIANAPOLIS NEWS, TUESDAY, MAY 16, 1905.

MRS. OLIVER P. MORTON CELEBRATES BIRTHDAY AT FOURSCORE YEARS

Widow of Indiana's Famous War Governor Spends Day in Richmond With Her Brother, John Burbank.

MRS. O. P. MORTON.

To-day is the eightieth anniversary of the birthday of Mrs. Oliver P. Morton, widow of Indiana's war Governor, and she is spending the day in Richmond with her brother, John Burbank, and her sisters, Mrs. Scott and Mrs. S. C. Gill, in the handsome new home of Mr. Burbank. Mrs. Morton is one of the most distinguished women in Indiana. She is much beloved by her circle of friends for her charm of manner and graciousness. She is keenly alert to important questions of the day and is a great reader, keeping abreast of the news in the daily papers, and she reads many books. Recently in her reading she returned to historical subjects. Mrs. Morton last year designed her own plans and made all the business arrangements in building her new home at 616 East Twenty-first street, this city, where she and her sister, Mrs. Gill, live. She is accomplished as a needlewoman and within a few years has made elaborate embroidered table pieces for the members of her family and a few intimate friends. Mrs. Morton is one of the honorary members of the Daughters of the Revolution of the newly-named Anthony Wayne Chapter.

*The May 16, 1905 article from "The Indianapolis Journal" about Lucinda Morton's 80th birthday.*

*She is accomplished as a needlewoman and within the last few years has made elaborate embroidered table pieces for the members of her family and a few intimate friends. Mrs. Morton is one of the honorary members of the Daughters of the Revolution of the newly named Anthony Wayne chapter.*

*Portrait of Lucinda Morton.*

*William R. Holloway, brother-in-law and close family member to Oliver and Lucinda Morton.*

Lucinda and William Holloway carefully preserved the documents that belonged to Oliver P. They were in the safety deposit vaults of the Indiana Trust Company. In May 1906, Lucinda presented them to the Indiana State Library. Some of the war letters bear the signature of Abraham Lincoln to Morton, to whom there was a strong personal friendship.

After Lucinda gave the valuable historical papers to the State Library, a call went out from the Library for others who had historical material relating to the state, to consider giving them to the Library. No letter, notebook, or document was too humble for the Library to consider placing it or copies of it in the Library archives. Many valuable paper resources have been collected and preserved for future historians.

Mrs. Rachel Scott, Lucinda's sister, passed away in Richmond in 1906. Her brother, John Burbank, had died in 1905. Rachel's funeral was at her home, "Rose Hill," in West Richmond. Her two sisters, Lucinda Morton and Sarah Gill, and many other relatives attended the funeral. Her obituary said she was one of the most highly respected and best-known women of the city. Her death was due to a fall on the ice about a week before her death.

Another memorial to Oliver P. was in the works to be placed at the State House. In June 1904, the twenty-fifth annual Encampment of the Department of Indiana, Grand Army of the Republic, met in Winona, Indiana. It was an organization of soldiers who had served honorably during the Civil War. A memorial for Governor Oliver P. Morton was proposed, and it was adopted that a committee should present it to the Legislature of Indiana.

The proposal was accepted and an act was passed and signed by

*A letter from Mrs. Lucinda Morton thanking the G.A.R. for their "efforts to secure a worthy monument to the memory of my husband, Oliver Perry Morton" was published in the February 25, 1905 edition of the "Indianapolis News."*

**Letter of Mrs. Lucinda Morton.**

The text of the letter sent by Mrs. Lucinda Morton, widow of Oliver P. Morton, to the Indiana department commander of the G. A. R. relative to the monument provided for by the Legislature, is as follows: "Will you kindly express to the veterans my most sincere thanks and appreciation for their successful efforts to secure a worthy monument to the memory of my husband, Oliver Perry Morton. His well-known and unwearied efforts to take care of the soldiers in camp, and field, in sickness and privations and to look after their families during their absence, surely makes it a fitting tribute to him. I reiterate my thanks to all who contributed to its success."

the Governor on February 25, 1905. Money was appropriated and donations were collected. The contract for the statue was given to Indianapolis sculptor, Rudolph Schwartz. He was able to prepare clay models quickly, and after consulting with Mrs. Morton and others who knew the Governor well, the memorial was finished much quicker than other Morton statues. All the work was done in his studio and it was reported that the casting of the bronze was also done in Indianapolis, a skill which few cities in the country could boast.

Lucinda visited the sculptor in his studio several times and took great interest in the making of the model for the statue. She worked with the commission and gave her approval to the work. In fact, the commission would not accept the statue until Mrs. Morton, William Holloway, and other relatives approved it.

In early May 1907, Lucinda and Sarah visited friends in Anderson. The Anderson newspaper reported that Lucinda had passed her eighty-second birthday a few days before and that she was exceptionally well preserved and active. But when she returned home from her trip, she was very tired.

On May 30, Memorial Day, Lucinda attended the dedication of the General Henry W. Lawson Monument in Indianapolis. She was one of the honored guests that had been requested to attend by President

*President Theodore Roosevelt.*

Theodore Roosevelt. President Roosevelt, the principal speaker, spoke directly to Lucinda when he honored Governor Morton in his speech. He said, "Governor Morton was in the class of great men with Lincoln, and in his sphere he was the equal of the national hero."

General Lawson was the hero of several wars, including the Civil War, Spanish–American War, and the Philippines Campaign. He spent much of his life in Ohio, but was a student at the Methodist Episcopal College in Fort Wayne, Indiana when the Civil War broke out. The original site of the monument was at the Marion County Courthouse. In 1917, the monument was moved to Indianapolis' Garfield Park and rededicated.

Lucinda was exhausted from the excitement of the President's visit and the many events surrounding the Lawson Monument. Her weakened condition forced her to take to her bed. Even though she was ill, she was determined to attend the dedication and unveiling of the new Morton Memorial in June. A few days before the event,

William Holloway, now serving as the United States Consul in Halifax, Nova Scotia, arrived in the city. He had received an urgent telegram concerning Lucinda's health. Holloway was her close friend, advisor, and beloved relative. Holloway, himself advanced in years, had been Governor Morton's close friend and his private secretary during his first term as Governor. Holloway found Lucinda weak and feeble, but she seemed a little better the day after he arrived. She was awake and able to speak with her family.

The day of the unveiling of the Monument, Lucinda was failing. She had wanted to live long enough to take part in the parade as well as the dedication. Her doctor told the family that she was too ill to be moved. The family slipped quietly out of the house so as not to disturb her and left her in the care of the nurse. She slept most of the day and was not aware of what was happening.

The Morton family members that were seated on the podium for the dedication were Mrs. Sarah Gill; William Holloway; Mrs. John Morton, of California; Walter Morton, and his 8-year-old son Oliver Perry Throck Morton, of Hartford, Connecticut; and Mrs. Edward Holloway of Chicago. They did not take part in the parade, but went directly to the State House.

The unveiling ceremony on July 23, 1907, drew large crowds from around the state. The day began with a parade of carriages of dignitaries, veterans' organizations, and marching bands. The crowds gathered at the site of the Monument in front of the State House to hear the speeches and see the unveiling. The choice of the person to uncover the statue was left to the Morton family. Lucinda's choice was her young grandson, Oliver P. Morton, Walter's son.

A platform was erected near the Monument to seat the speakers, the family, and personal friends of Governor Morton, about fifty people. After a few words from men representing the Monument commission, the Governor of Indiana, Frank Hanley, gave the dedication speech. He reviewed Morton's public career and spoke of the "statesman's fearless but kindly character, his love for the Union and his work among the wounded Indiana soldiers in the field hospitals." In the days before microphones, orators had to project their voices over a large area. The newspaper story said Governor Hanley's voice was loud enough to be heard everywhere.

At the close of the speeches and music selections, it was time for the unveiling. Oliver P. Morton, the grandson of Governor Morton, pulled the mechanism that released the large 45-star flag covering the

UNVEILS MORTON MONUMENT

OLIVER PERRY THROCK MORTON.
Grandson of the Famous War Governor.

*Oliver Perry Morton, Walter's young son, unveiled the Morton statue in front of the Indiana State House in 1907. Courtesy of Indiana Historical Society.*

monument. Cheers and applause filled the air for many minutes.

Lucinda could not attend the ceremony but everyone knew of her approval. In September 1906, while she was still able, Lucinda had written a letter to the commission. She congratulated the commission and spoke of her appreciation of their work on behalf of her husband. She added her praise for the statue.

> *I think the statue is magnificent in every particular and the likeness is as near perfect as it is possible to make in plaster, and altogether a worthy testimonial for his services to state and country.*
>
> *In behalf of myself and family, I express to you my most earnest thanks.*
>
> *Sincerely yours,*
>
> *Lucinda M. Morton*

Lucinda rallied enough to say goodbye to her son Walter and her grandson Oliver before they left Indianapolis. Walter could not know when his mother might pass away. When they left, she went into a deep sleep and died peacefully on July 28, 1907, just five days after the unveiling of the Monument. Several Indiana newspapers and many out-of-state newspapers carried the story of her death. The *East Oregonian* of Pendleton, Oregon printed her obituary. Her grandson, Oliver P. Morton, John's son, who had unveiled the Circle Park statue of his grandfather, was a reclamation lawyer in Pendleton.

Lucinda's funeral was held on July 31, 1907, at the Central Christian Church in Indianapolis. Her longtime friend and pastor, Rev. Dr. Daniel R. Lucas, conducted the services. Her son Walter was able to return for the funeral, and her family in Indianapolis, Centerville, and Richmond attended. She was buried in Crown Hill Cemetery next to her husband.

Sarah Gill had lived with Lucinda for many years and was the beneficiary of her will. Lucinda had given away or disposed of most of her things while she was alive. She left the house and whatever money was left to Sarah.

Sarah was in her late seventies. She kept the house and her brother-in-law, William Holloway, came to live with her. In February 1908, Sarah had a cataract operation on her eye. When she returned home, she seemed better. She had been instructed to be careful not to get upset or take any chances of allowing a tear to come to her eye. But nervous exhaustion came on her and she was not in a condition to fight it. She passed away barely seven months after her sister, Lucinda. Sarah was buried in Crown Hill Cemetery in Indianapolis, next to her

*The gravesite of the Oliver P. Morton family. The small stones in front are for Oliver P. Morton and Lucinda M. Morton. The tall memorial and small stone at the center are for Sarah Gill and her daughter, Josephine. All of the Morton children are interred here except John. He died and was buried on St. Paul Island, Alaska. His memorial is marked here. Courtesy of C. Bedford Crenshaw.*

daughter, Josephine. Both graves are located at the Morton gravesite with Oliver P. and family. William Holloway and his wife, Eliza, are also buried close by.

Only two of Lucinda's siblings were still living, her brothers, Major Jacob E. Burbank of Maiden, Massachusetts, and Joseph H. Burbank of Decatur, Nebraska. There were several nieces and nephews.

The story of the Indiana's Civil War Governor's wife had come to an end. The obituary in the *Richmond Palladium* described her life well. It was titled "Was Great Aid to Husband."

> *No Indianapolis woman, perhaps had gone through so many and varied experiences as Mrs. Lucinda M. Morton.*
>
> *The wife of Indiana's war governor, Mrs. Morton took a keen interest in everything that interested her husband in those stormy days, even accompanying him on his political campaigns. This interest in all of his affairs she maintained until his death in 1877, accompanying him on his trips to California, Mexico, Oregon and other places. She was an inveterate reader and always kept abreast of the times.*

Lucinda M. Morton was a woman to be admired. She did not appear to complain and did her best to care for those around her. She lived an interesting life but never tried to take advantage of her social position for her own gain. Her legacy was of friendship, love, and devotion to family and friends. A true love story between a husband and wife, Oliver P. Morton spoke the truth about his wife when he said, "She never failed me."

# INDEX

**A**



**B**

**C**



**D**

# ABOUT THE AUTHOR CAROLYN LAFEVER

*Carolyn Lafever.*

Carolyn Lafever has been writing professionally since 1975. She published her first book, *The Murals of Charles Newcomb, A Story of Hagerstown, Indiana* in 1993. Mrs. Lafever has served on the Board of Trustees for three Historical Societies in Wayne County, and was the first director of the Hagerstown Museum. She gave many hours to volunteering as a docent, preparing exhibits, and as collection manager for the Historic Mansion House in Centerville.

In 2000, Mrs. Lafever was appointed the Wayne County Historian by the Indiana Historical Society. She retired from that position in 2020, becoming the Wayne County Historian Emeritus.

From 1998, she authored several books and articles about the history of Wayne County and Indiana. Her articles have appeared in the *Indianapolis Star Magazine; Traces of Indiana and Midwestern History;* and *Antique Week.* For ten years she was the feature writer for the monthly magazine of the *Palladium–Item* newspaper in

Richmond, Indiana.

Wayne County celebrated 200 years in 2010. To commemorate the event, Mrs. Lafever wrote *Wayne County, Indiana, The Battles for the Courthouse.* She was contributing editor for Centerville's 200$^{th}$ anniversary book, *Through the Arches of Time* in 2014. This latest book about Lucinda Burbank Morton was a four-and-one-half-year project.

Mrs. Lafever is a graduate of Ball State, Muncie, Indiana, with a Masters Degree in music education.

She and her husband, Edward, live in Cambridge City, Indiana. They are the parents of four children, and have seven grandchildren and six great-grandchildren. Although she has accomplished many things, her first loves are her faith, her home, and family.

Made in the USA
Columbia, SC
11 August 2024

0389be42-3fd8-463e-9020-d22c5ab39b1bR01